I0434269

Race, Education and the Continuing American Dilemma

Race, Education and the Continuing American Dilemma

"The story of one people's fight against pain, power, and the politics of the South."

Eric O. Rogers, Ph.D.

iUniverse, Inc.
New York Lincoln Shanghai

Race, Education and the Continuing American Dilemma
"The story of one people's fight against pain, power, and the politics of the
South."

All Rights Reserved © 2004 by Eric O. Rogers, Ph.D.

No part of this book may be reproduced or transmitted in any form or by
any means, graphic, electronic, or mechanical, including photocopying,
recording, taping, or by any information storage retrieval system, without the
written permission of the publisher.

iUniverse, Inc.

For information address:
iUniverse, Inc.
2021 Pine Lake Road, Suite 100
Lincoln, NE 68512
www.iuniverse.com

ISBN: 0-595-33274-9

Printed in the United States of America

To by beloved father, hero and mentor, the late *Dallas Minor Rogers, Sr.*, (9/18/15/-2/8/77).

To my beloved mother, heroine and mentor, the late *Bernice King Rogers* (5/16/18-1/21/04).

CONTENTS

LIST OF TABLES

PREFACE

Life is unfair. The reality of the world in which we live in dictates that as we grow old, mysteries unfold. Stranger than fiction is the reality that education has always been an expensive thing. The United Negro College Fund 1970's slogan " A mind is a terrible thing to waste," seems inescapably true regardless of the times. When one begins to survey the historical scene, it is impossible to ignore the fact that Thomas Jefferson, the 3rd president and the architect of the Preamble and the Declaration of Independence, valued education, freedom and the right of people to govern themselves freely. He further argued that "we hold these truths to be self evident, that all men are created equal and born with certain unalienable rights that among these are the right to life, liberty and the pursuit of happiness-" Equally important, the 18th century philosopher, Ralph Waldo Emerson, once said in a Harvard lecture, back in 1871, that " if a man can write a better book, preach a better sermon, or make a mousetrap better than his neighbor, though he builds his house in the woods, the world will make a beaten path unto his door."

It is upon these premises that many people of color stake their claim in these United States of America that education is the ticket to both freedom, success and privileges afforded only to the few. Even when it was a crime to teach slaves to read, their ancestors, were willing and far too often, able to die thirsting for a greater knowledge, tasting for a higher learning and fasting to see, to feel, and to experience a different world view than the one they knew. The plot thickens as history unravels with concise and critical sightings of how they crossed rivers, climbed mountains, walked through valleys and endured the cold, callous and cynical, albeit, castrating and disenfranchising impact of black codes, lynchings, segregation and double standards in order to obtain an invaluable and endless education.

Equally important, HBCUs (Historically Black Colleges and Universities) were founded in the 1800s to meet the educational needs of African-Americans during a time in which they were denied admission to traditional White institutions (TWIs). At a time when many schools barred their doors to blacks and other people of color, these colleges (HBCUs) offered many times, the best and the only opportunities for a higher education. While recognizing that there are still continuing legal, educational policy and social issues that remain unclear about the role of HBCUs, questions still remain about their uniqueness and effectiveness. Today, many of the past and historical barriers have been brought down by the law, social change and desegregation litigation. But court rulings and subsequent legal battels have not left a clear signal or a conclusive end to the role and future of HBCUs.

Subsequently, not all have been able to benefit directly from these institutions. Far too many have suffered, bled and died with nothing gained, but everything essentially lost. And yet there are others who have suffered, struggled and sacrificed and seen little profit from their experiences. Nevertheless, many have benefited and to those who did, their descendants are a shining example of history, hope and healing beautifully interwoven in the fabric of American life. Their successes are evidence that HBCUs offer values and victories despite obstacles. This publication is the story of their saga, their struggles and their successes against the pains, the powers and the politics of the South.

CHAPTER ONE

Introduction

Historically black colleges and universities (HBCUs) grew up within the United States to meet the educational needs of African-Americans during an era in which they found themselves denied admission to institutions accepting only white students. Such origins by definition dictated that the HBCUs became the first means of providing postsecondary education to black students. Moreover, throughout the early years of affirmative action, HBCUs provided the only mode through which black students could reliably achieve higher education. With the advent of desegregation legislation designed to provide access and opportunity for African-Americans to attend historically white institutions, the status of, and the continuing need for, the HBCU came under scrutiny and into question.

In filing desegregation litigation, HBCUs simply sought to gain access to funds historically denied but necessary for their survival and effectiveness. These institutions sought to raise their standards, provide quality learning and upgrade their facilities to fulfill their respective missions while meeting the needs of their African-American constituents. Gradually, the HBCUs began to face controversial challenges both in the courts and in their respective communities that threatened their continued existence.

A significant turning point in the history of higher education occurred in 1975 when the U.S. Supreme Court addressed itself to the desegregation case, *United States* v. *Fordice*. In this case, the State of Mississippi's postsecondary institutions of higher learning presented a history of segregative practices and policies still dominant. The facts in *Fordice* revolve around Mississippi's efforts to continue a long-established policy of *de jure* segregation in its public university system maintaining "five almost completely white and three almost exclusively black universities" (*Fordice*, p. 2729). Jackson State University, the state's largest and most progressive HBCU, became the primary center of conflict when relatives of students attending the institution complained of discrimination in the form of inadequate educational instruction and facilities offered by the State of Mississippi.

A group of private citizens, mostly African-Americans, sued the governor of Mississippi for alleged racial discrimination in the state university system. The United States government intervened, claiming that state officials had failed to dismantle this dual system in violation of the Equal Protection Clause of the Fourteenth Amendment and Title VI of the Civil Rights Act of 1964. Although the Supreme Court had addressed this dual system question directly only at the elementary and secondary levels, the obligation to dismantle dual systems of education applied to higher education as well. From the onset, the Court made clear its position in *Fordice* that Mississippi had a constitutional duty to dismantle its segregated programs. The primary issue before the Court was whether or not the state had met its affirmative duty to dismantle its prior dual university system (*Fordice*, p. 2735). In its view, Mississippi's mere adoption and implementation of race-neutral policies to govern its system of higher education did not fulfill this affirmative duty.

The state, on other hand, argued that it had met this affirmative duty when it abolished laws requiring separate education of the races and when the universities changed their admissions policies allowing minorities to be enrolled. It further maintained that, unlike elementary and secondary school children, university students can choose "totally unfettered" which university they wish to attend. Therefore, the Court in *Fordice,* also had to consider the issue of choice.

Unlike the earlier decisions, however, choice alone did not dictate the *Fordice* Court's opinion. The Court held that the choice issue is determinant only when a state has not fostered segregation by playing a part in students' decisions. The Court went on to identify four polices of the Mississippi public university system that were "constitutionally suspect." The first of these had to do with admission standards that (a) proved discriminatory intent because they were traceable to the former *de jure* system, and (b) had discriminatory effects because they were based solely on the American College Testing Program (ACT) cut-off scores. Not only did African-American Students score lower on these tests, but the minimum score for admission was higher at the predominantly white universities in Mississippi (*Fordice*, p. 2739).

A second policy scrutinized by the Court was Mississippi's classification scheme for institutional mission. Three of the predominantly white universities were designated as "flagship" institutions. They offered the most advanced programs and the broadest curricula offerings and therefore received more funds than the other institutions. The state's historically black institutions, on the other hand, were much more limited in their missions and, consequently, in their funding. New mission designations for the state's universities, adopted in 1981, still reflected old policies based on *de jure* segregation. Third, the Court questioned the policy of "unnecessary duplication" of programs between Mississippi's historically white and historically black institutions. Unnecessary duplication was instances in which two or more institutions offered the same nonessential or non-core program. It maintained that this policy of duplication was directly tied to the previous separate-but-equal notion that supported the dual system of *de jure* segregation *(Fordice, p. 2740)*.

Lastly, the Court focused on the state's need to maintain all eight universities in light of limited financial resources and proximate geographical locations *(Fordice, p. 2741)*. This issue raised fears among many that Mississippi might eliminate its HBCUs as a means of meeting its affirmative duty to desegregate. Although the Court stated explicitly that this did not mean that any of the schools would necessarily have to be abandoned, its language clearly leaves the decision with state officials and academicians.

Equally important is that the *Fordice* case was filed in 1975 after the State of Mississippi had failed for several years to submit an acceptable desegregation plan to the U.S. Department of Health, Education and Welfare. After 12 years of unsuccessful negotiations, the trial ensued. In the subsequent years of litigation, *Fordice* became viewed as a victory for desegregation efforts, but the late Jake Ayers and other private plaintiffs may have lost or not reached their original goals. They had sought an order that would have required upgrading Mississippi's HBCUs. What they wanted, in effect, was remedy reminiscent of the "equalization" relief sought in the pre-Brown cases. The Court refused to endorse this approach. It found that a separate but "more equal" system would not satisfy the state's duty to dismantle its segregated educational system. At the conclusion of its opinion, the Court indicated that increasing funding for HBCUs might be necessary to achieve complete disestablishment of the segregated system. This suggests that the Court would endorse upgrading HBCUs only if doing so would attract white students and operate to eliminate the racial identifiability of the institutions. Further igniting this controversy is the irony that because of *Fordice*, the institutions that once sustained blacks during segregation are now becoming subject to dismantling in an effort to combat its vestiges. Despite the assurances and statements supported by the *Fordice* Court, some scholars remain skeptical. The fear remains that HBCUs will be inevitable casualties of higher-education desegregation, further limiting the academic and professional opportunities of historically disadvantaged populations.

Fordice enforcement became difficult because the standard it set leaves the future of publicly funded HBCUs in considerable doubt. In addition, three

HBCUs in the state saw in the opinion a potential for their own discontinuance. Jackson State University, the state's largest and most progressive HBCU, became the primary center of conflict when its constituents filed suit alleging discrimination in the form of inadequate educational instruction and facilities offered by the State of Mississippi.

In *Fordice*, the Court addressed the issue of "whether states that maintained racially segregated systems of higher education are obligated to take steps beyond adopting race-neutral admissions policies to desegregate their educational institutions." The Court answered this question in the affirmative and decided that race-neutral policies alone are insufficient to rectify the effects of prior *de jure* segregation. The Court further adopted a standard requiring states to eliminate all policies that continue to exert a discriminatory effect and are traceable to a *de jure* system.

The *Fordice* ruling inspired controversy because it threatened the future existence of HBCUs. *Fordice* required state legislatures to eliminate single-race based schools unless they could provide legal or educational justification for their continued existence. This new orientation applied, moreover, not just in Mississippi but also nationwide, with ramifications for all other HBCUs. For the first time, the Court had specifically set the standard for any and all current and future decisions regarding the continuance of public HBCUs; their very futures had essentially to be weighed against the *Fordice* ruling.

In the study presented here, the principal roles include the Mississippi State Legislature's Council on Higher Learning, Jackson State University and its constituents—all of which have a compelling interest in terms of Mississippi's HBCUs continuing their existence. Other problems embedded within the dilemma center around the terms, the contexts and the control limits or restrictions that figure to emerge. If these issues go without a critical assessment, the remaining option is to discontinue Jackson State University.

With *Fordice* setting the current standards, each party must find the means and methods to justify existence for Mississippi's HBCUs and particularly Jackson State University.

On April 23, 2002, after years of desegregation litigation in Mississippi, the U.S. Supreme Court took the unusual step of settling a 27-year-old desegregation lawsuit for one particular HBCU, Jackson State University. In essence, once the dust had cleared, the Court required the State of Mississippi to provide $500 million to its three HBCUs over a period of 17 years, primarily for academic programs, support services and minority scholarships and to upgrade their facilities. But the Court's judgment hardly constituted a conclusive end. The Court failed to define a current or future role for Jackson State University or shed any conclusive light on the likelihood of its very continuance. It simply compensated Mississippi's three HBCUs with money denied and owed as a result of persistent racism. The unresolved issues continue to fuel debate over the future of Jackson State University and its ability to serve the citizens of Mississippi. This study addresses some of the questions and issues raised in *Fordice* and explores the ensuing debate.

One can place the current debate over the HBCU into two camps. In the first camp are those who promote the continuation of the HBCUs, arguing that a wealth of evidence suggests that HBCUs continue to fill a unique role in higher education and provide assistance for African-American students and communities in meeting the racial and equity challenges in the twenty-first century.

Dr. Elias Blake Jr.—formerly President of an HBCU, Clark College in Atlanta—and now Director of the Washington, D.C.-based Benjamin E. Mays Center, believes that HBCUs continue to provide unique educational and social opportunities to disadvantaged and historically underrepresented populations in search of higher learning not normally available to them at predominantly white institutions. For Blake, HBCUs have produced numerous African-Americans who have become professionals in underrepresented fields traditionally closed to them like science, math, engineering and medicine. Without HBCUs, they would have been unlikely to achieve these positions (Jaschik, 1999). Blake further recommends laws to safeguard the survival of HBCUs and maintain their unique contributions to society.

Dr. James D. Anderson (1999), Professor of Education at the University of Illinois and author of the book, *The Education of Blacks in the South, 1860-1935*, suggests that HBCUs offer invaluable conditions and opportunities for educating and training unique people "against the odds." According to Anderson, HBCUs provide the climate and support systems that encourage outstanding achievements among minorities locked out of higher education for decades. Secondly, they are crucial to society because their evolution reflects the triumphs and the tragedies of the larger African-American experience. These institutions are vital because they convey black thought, black life and black interest from black perspectives unheard and unseen through the white experience (Anderson, 1999). Meanwhile, Dr. Kenneth Tollett (1994), Professor and former Dean of the Howard University Law School and another expert on HBCUs, sees these institutions as providing enclaves for inter-and intra-racial relationships for the larger society. Moreover, HBCUs preserve African-American history, culture and traditions. Equally important, at HBCUs minorities and non-traditional whites can observe and appreciate African-Americans as leaders and as role models preparing students for leadership in society and their communities.

The second camp, those who oppose HBCUs, suggest that a racially based school for the African-American student becomes irrelevant when all schools become willing to provide access to black students as well as students of other minority groups. Many of the social norms that fostered and perpetuated the inception of the HBCUs (e.g., "separate but equal" policies) are now passe, thereby lessening the argument in favor of the continued existence of HBCUs. Robert Davis (1996), Professor of Law at the University of Mississippi, advocates closing, merging or consolidating HBCUs because a degree from an HBCU has a "crippling effect" on the graduate as he or she enters the job market. For Davis, those who argue for the survival of HBCUs would sacrifice "the need for quality of education" for the effort simply to "preserve certain interests of today" and the radical changes required in higher education today include the elimination of "inferior schools."

Dr. F. Kent Wyatt (1997), former President of the historically white Delta State University, suggests that as equal access is now available to all, Mississippi should be moving toward a single, unitary system of higher education because more people stand a chance to benefit from such a regularized system. Finally, Senator Eugene J. Watts, Chairman of the Education Subcommittee of the U.S. Senate Finance Committee, recently raised an important discussion about the role and future of HBCUs: "We spend a great deal of time and money in all of our institutions to increase our minority participation. But it is absolutely counterproductive to maintain a separate black institution. Either you believe in integration or you don't. Let's not try to have it both ways. HBCUs have served their purpose and it's time to move on" (Hebel, 2001, p. 16).

Purpose of the Study

The study reported here evaluated the strength of the two foregoing positions on the survival of HBCUs by relying on a case history of higher education in Mississippi, focusing in particular on Jackson State University. This researcher sought to explore the literature on HBCUs with the intention of determining and clarifying evidence that justifies or calls into question the continued existence of Jackson State University. This study further sought to explore the two positions by investigating institutional effectiveness at Jackson State University in terms of such key performance indicators as enrollment trends, graduation rates, degree completions, mission statements and instructional programs.

"Institutional effectiveness" denotes the process of assessing how well the college fulfills its mission and mandate (e.g., the legislative mandate and accreditation standards), that is to say, how well it is doing what it is supposed to do, including how well its constituents are learning and how well its administrative and educational support services support its mission (Cohen, 1994). Some of the most widely recognized and effective strategies for addressing institutional effectiveness include analyzing general education outcomes and providing operational and strategic planning, program implementation, pre- and post-measures of student learning, surveys, institutional self-study reports, interviews, accreditation and accountability reports (Gentemann, 1989). Further, one typically expresses these reports in terms of quantitative and qualitative indicators (Todd, 1998).

The exploration of institutional effectiveness at Jackson State University followed a historical descriptive approach designed to examine higher education for African-Americans within Mississippi in the years following desegregation and to determine the extent to which the educational opportunities Jackson State University provided and enhanced the employment possibilities for its students. In addition, this researcher analyzed the perceptions among key administrators and staff members at Jackson State University in terms of the impact of desegregation to determine if a sociological benefit flowed from attending an HBCU and whether any related evidence seemed to justify its continued existence.

Finally, this study collected and weighed the issues and conditions that currently appear to validate or invalidate Jackson State University's role in providing African-American students with educational opportunities.

Institutional and Legal Context of the Study

This researcher decided to compile a case history of Jackson State University on the grounds that Jackson State University offered a particularly compelling case for evaluating the two positions on the survival of HBCUs. More specifically, Jackson State University became the focus of a desegregation effort in higher education that had never before been approached on a national level. *Fordice* compelled the Supreme Court to determine that the State of Mississippi continued to promote segregation within its postsecondary educational programs, and it was the first federal court case to approach the nature of desegregation within higher education with respect to traditionally white versus HBCU institutions. Until this point, the cases had addressed only K-12 education desegregation. The facts and resulting rulings of *Fordice*, centered as they were on Jackson State University, set the national stage for debate, dialogue and decisions that would have far-reaching implications for other HBCUs both in Mississippi and other southern states.

The Justices hearing *United States* v. *Fordice* formulated three tests for clarifying whether a system was still segregated (*U.S. v. Fordice* 50 U.S. 120 Led 2d 575):

1. Was there duplication of resources and programs between institutions?

2. Were institutions ethnically homogeneous?

3. Were the institutions able to justify the reasons for resource duplication and

4. the homogeneous state of school population?

The Court held that the defendant, the State of Mississippi, had failed the first two tests since their five traditionally white institutions (TWIs) within Mississippi remained predominantly white while the HBCUs remained predominantly black, and course duplications existed between the two types of institutions—indications that Mississippi intended its TWIs and HBCUs to remain segregated. The Court required Mississippi either to justify the continued existence of its HBCUs or eliminate them. No discussion centered on whether any TWI should be justified or eliminated.

To validate the continuation of the HBCUs, one must apply the Court's third test—that justification for reasons of separation. The reader should note, at this point, that this study addresses the justification of continued program maintenance and potential restructuring at Jackson State University and no other HBCU, and it focuses on information pertaining mainly to this one institution. Therefore, one must resist drawing firm conclusions about any other HBCU. Nonetheless, in exploring the justification for the continuance or discontinuance of Jackson State University, this study demonstrates those various qualities found within this specific institution that may exist and can similarly be explored within other HBCUs.

In the aftermath of the Supreme Court's decision, the fact that Mississippi had continued segregation in its institutions of higher learning seems to have been lost. Still, the need for justification seems destined to have significant consequences for the HBCUs. Many states have begun to comply with the decision, implementing various proposals for changes in admissions criteria, mergers and closures. For example, Mississippi raised entrance requirements at its three HBCUs, which resulted in enrollment declines ranging from 9.9% to 20.1% (Healy, 1996). In addition, while the HBCUs affected were public institutions, *U.S. v. Fordice* also posed a threat to private HBCUs by influencing their funding. Most private HBCUs depend heavily on a combination of federal funding and private donations to promote curriculum enrichment and student endowments. Without this funding, enrollment at the private HBCUs promises to shrink, thereby threatening their longevity.

Finally, the specter of mergers and closures puts pressure on HBCUs to provide educational justification for their continued existence. Doing so involves returning to the historical debates between Washington and DuBois at the beginning of the last century (Lemelle, 2002). We turn now to these questions—How much desegregation allows HBCUs to justify their continued existence—that we now turn.

Research Questions to Be Answered

While many subsidiary questions affect the overall purpose of this study, the foremost research question addressed is: What evidence exists to justify the continued existence of HBCUs? This study clearly presents and critically assesses the evidence that answers this research question.

To answer the primary research question, this researcher had to raise numerous other questions. Though subsidiary, these additional questions promoted the original research goal. Further, to determine if, after desegregation and the gradual opening of white schools to black students, a need remained for African-Americans to gain access to the educational opportunities. A secondary research question emerged: What has been the impact of desegregation on one particular HBCU, Jackson State University, in terms of institutional effectiveness relating to the key performance indicators? This researcher relied on the following five performance indicators:

1. Mission Assignments,

2. Admission Enrollment and Headcounts,

3. Graduation Rates,

4. Degree Completions, and

5. Instructional Programs.

This researcher used performance indicators to assess the extent to which the missions, operations and outcomes changed within Jackson State University after desegregation and the extent to which they validate its continuance or discontinuance. These indicators also served, in part, to suggest whether or not there is enough evidence to justify its continued existence or extinction in the context of the current political and social climate that seeks to dismantle admission restrictions on the basis of race. Equally important, interviews with administrators who directly influenced the institutional effectiveness plans and practices at Jackson State University provided this researcher with a unique internal perspective on the impact of desegregation on Jackson State University.

After addressing the primary and secondary questions, the study moved on to qualify the contexts in which HBCUs ought to continue their operations. For instance, the study enumerates the particular kinds of programs HBCUs should provide in the twenty-first century; the kinds of sociological and cultural benefits that support educational and career success for an HBCU student; and the particular ways in which HBCUs should maneuver given the prevailing political, economic and social climate within the U.S. Towards this qualification, this researcher formulated these four questions:

1. Should HBCUs exist and, if so, in what contexts?

2. What kind of modern education should an HBCU provide?

3. How should an HBCU relate to the dominant, political, economic and social environment in the U.S.?

4. Is there a sociological benefit to students attending an HBCU in terms of academic preparation, culture and achievement prospects?

By analyzing the historical impact of desegregation on Jackson State University, one can draw inferences that provide several bases for predicting the future institutional effectiveness of Jackson State University and, quite possibly, other HBCUs as well.

Nature and Format of this Study

This researcher intends to promote a sociological understanding of the perceptions and views of various influential individuals at Jackson State University. The methodology of a descriptive case study was chosen as the best means for documenting the effects of desegregation on Jackson State University. The interviews and institutional data spanned the years from 1975 to 2002 and were used to analyze, assess and evaluate the desegregation impact in terms of the institutional effectiveness Jackson State University experienced in those years.

The descriptive case study methodology invited a thorough exploration into the "how" and "why" of various factors that caused an ascertainable impact on the University in question (Yin, 1994).

Combining interviews and an analysis of published data into a descriptive case study increases our understanding of both the qualities currently embodied by Jackson State University and the information that points to possible change. The format of the discussion follows.

Chapter One introduces the HBCUs and sets forth the background rationale and purpose of the study as well as the reasons for its focus on Jackson State University.

Chapter Two discusses the origin of HBCUs and their struggle for survival against numerous challenges, obstacles and other impinging factors. The chapter also presents a summary of federal case rulings and other social factors that generated desegregation nationally and specifically in Mississippi from the 1800s to the present. Further, the chapter explores Mississippi's postsecondary education system, its own defined criteria for institutional effectiveness, the history of black education in Mississippi and the case of *United States* v. *Fordice.*

Chapter Three provides a methodological basis for exploring the central research question: What evidence exists to justify the continuation or the discontinuation of HBCUs? The research described here identified quantitative factors on the basis of system-wide and institutional statistical data comparing Jackson State University and Mississippi's TWIs in terms of key performance indicators (enrollment, mission assignments, graduation rates). Equally important, the chapter includes the qualitative data consisted of interviews with Mississippi higher education authorities and Jackson State University's administrative officials and staff who experienced and appraised the impact of desegregation between 1975 and 2002 in Mississippi.

Chapter Four presents the findings along with summary discussions and analyses. The interpretations there explain the findings of the quantitative and qualitative research data. Other questions or issues that emerged during the research also receive attention in this section along with their implications and importance to the research focus. This chapter also discusses the significance of the study and the inferences one can draw regarding the impact of desegregation, with an emphasis on the findings of the research regarding what evidence exists to justify the continued existence of Jackson State University and, by extension, other HBCUs.

Chapter Five provides an overview and conclusion regarding the findings of the study and the attendant prospects for the continuation or the discontinuance of Jackson State University. Further, this researcher makes specific recommendations regarding the future role of Jackson State University and offers suggestions for additional research.

CHAPTER TWO

Review of Literature

Historically Black Colleges and Universities in Light of Desegregation

To obtain reliable evidence about the wisdom of continuing HBCUs, one must also consider the environment and the attendant social, economic, and political factors that gave rise to HBCUs in the first place, including the various dilemmas and challenges they faced then and have faced over the years. Thus, one should explore the historical, legal and policy issues and the national demographics applicable to HBCUs to understand fully their origins and their struggle for survival in the education marketplace. This chapter clarifies these points with respect to the historically black Jackson State University. In addition, one must examine the history of black education in Mississippi to contextualize the relevance of Jackson State University in relation to the Supreme Court's decision to desegregate higher education in Mississippi. This chapter examines the following five topics:

1. The historical origin of HBCUs,

2. The issue of desegregation, the current status of HBCUs and relevant policy implications,

3. Mississippi's higher education system,

4. The history of black education in Mississippi, and

5. *Fordice* and its relationship to Jackson State University.

Origin and History of HBCUs, 1837-2002

Historically black colleges and universities were established to serve the educational needs of African-Americans in a time when they were denied admission to traditionally white institutions, or TWIs (Bush, 1991). Responding directly to the segregation of other institutions of higher learning, the HBCUs became the principal means for providing postsecondary education primarily to disenfranchised African-Americans. Indeed, even former President George Bush Sr. described the unique mission of historically black colleges and universities:

At a time when many schools barred their doors to black Americans, these colleges offered the best, and often the only, opportunities for a higher education. Today, thank heaven, most of those barriers have been brought down by the law, and yet historically black colleges and universities still represent a vital component of American higher education (Bush, 1991, p. 17).

Separate but Equal

This "vital component" of the educational scheme within America is actually a comparatively recent event in the history of the country. Prior to the Civil War, no structured higher education systems existed for black students in the United States. Public policy and certain statutory provisions prohibited the education of blacks, regardless of their age, in several regions of the nation (Anderson, 1988). The first higher education institution for blacks, the Institute for Colored Youth, was founded in Cheyney, Pennsylvania in 1837 and was soon followed by two other black institutions, Lincoln University in Pennsylvania (1854) and Wilberforce University in Ohio (1856).

Although these institutions were referred to as "universities and institutes" from their founding, a major part of their mission in the early years was to provide elementary and secondary schooling for black students who had no previous education. Not until the early 1900s did most HBCUs begin to offer courses and programs at the postsecondary level (Anderson, 1988). Public support for higher education for black students was reflected in the enactment of the second Morrill Act in 1890, requiring states with racially segregated public higher education systems to provide a land-grant institution for black students whenever a land-grant institution for white students was restricted to white students. After the passage of the Act, public land-grant institutions specifically for blacks appeared in each of the Southern and border states. As a result, some entirely new public black institutions were founded while a number of private black schools came under public control. Eventually, 16 black institutions were designated as land-grant colleges (Garibaldi, 1984). Like their white counterparts, these institutions offered courses in agricultural, mechanical and industrial subjects but few offered college level-courses and awarded degrees.

One of the key legal issues complicating the inception of these institutions designated for black students was the Supreme Court's ruling in the case of *Plessy* v. *Ferguson* (1896). This decision established a "separate but equal" doctrine in public accommodations. In brief, the court's decision reflected the general social perception following the Civil War that the races may be "equals." This equality could be fairly accomplished through providing separate facilities for both blacks and whites. Within education, this belief gave rise to separate schools for blacks and whites, a form of legally sanctioned segregation. This public elementary and secondary schooling system encouraged black colleges to focus on teacher training to prepare a pool of instructors for segregated schools. At the same time, the expansion of black secondary schools reduced the need for black colleges to provide college-preparatory instruction. In 1953, HBCUs enrolled more than 32,000 students in such private black institutions as Fisk University, Spelman College and Tuskeegee Institute, as well as a host of other smaller black colleges in the Southern border states. In the same year, more than 43,000 students were enrolled in public black colleges. HBCUs had also enrolled 3,200 students in graduate programs. These private and public institutions served the important mission of providing education for teachers, ministers, lawyers and doctors for the black population in a racially segregated society (Bullock, 1967).

The addition of graduate programs offered primarily at the public HBCUs represented an official response to three specific decisions the Supreme Court made in *Plessy*, applying the separate but equal doctrine to establish graduate and professional education.

1. A state must offer schooling for blacks when it provides such for whites *(Sipuel* v. *Board of Regents of the University of California,* 1948).

2. Black students must receive the same treatment as white students in school *(McLaurin* v. *Oklahoma State Regents,* 1950).

3. A state must provide facilities of comparable quality for black and white students *(Sweatt* v. *Painter,* 1950). Black students increasingly were admitted into some traditionally white graduate and professional schools if their program of study was unavailable at HBCUs. In effect then, desegregation in higher education began at the post-baccalaureate level (Coleman, 1990).

The Advent of Desegregation

Within a comparatively brief time, after black HBCU graduates began to appear in white graduate programs, the U.S. Supreme Court decision in *Brown v. Board of Education* (1954) reversed the separate but equal doctrine and held racially segregated public schools to be inherently unequal and deprived black children of equal protection guaranteed by the Fourteenth Amendment of the Constitution. Despite the landmark decision, however, most HBCUs remained segregated and were forced to function with substandard facilities and budgets. Lack of adequate libraries and scientific research and financial resources placed a serious burden on many HBCUs and several of the public HBCUs closed or merged with TWIs. But most black college students in the South continued to attend HBCUs years after the *Brown* decision was rendered (Myers, 1989).

Ten years following the decision in *Brown,* Congress enacted Title VI of the Civil Rights Act to provide a mechanism for ensuring equal opportunity in federally assisted programs and institutions. In enacting Title VI, Congress also reflected its concern with the slow progress in desegregating educational institutions following the Supreme Court's ruling in *Brown.* Title VI protects individuals from discrimination based on race, color and national origin in programs or activities receiving federal financial assistance. Passage of this law led to the establishment of the Office for Civil Rights (OCR) in the former Department of Health, Education and Welfare (Office for Civil Rights, 1991). In the 1960s and early 1970s, OCR placed its emphasis on compliance in eliminating unconstitutional elementary and secondary school segregation in the Southern border states (Office for Civil Rights, 1991).

At the time Title VI was enacted, 19 states were found to be operating racially segregated higher education systems. In 1969-70, after intensive investigative work, OCR notified a number of these states that they were in violation for having failed to dismantle their segregated systems of higher education. While OCR sought to promote statewide higher education desegregation plans, its efforts went almost entirely without success. Consequently, in 1970 private plaintiffs filed suit against HEW for failing to initiate enforcement action against the systems under investigation by OCR. In 1977, as part of what became known as the *Adams* case, the Court ordered the federal government to establish new uniform criteria for statewide desegregation.

In response, OCR published "Criteria Specifying the Ingredients of Acceptable Plans to Desegregate State Systems of Public Higher Education" (Office for Civil Rights, 1991). "The Criteria," as it was called, recognized the unique role of HBCUs in meeting the educational needs of black students and called for the enhancement of HBCUs through improvements in physical plants and equipment, in the quality of their faculties, in their libraries and in the financial support they received. The Criteria also called for expanding non-minority enrollment at HBCUs by offering academic programs in high demand or unavailable on the other state campuses. Efforts began to provide HBCUs with resources comparable to those at traditionally white institutions having similar missions.

Under the plans accepted by OCR, HBCUs have aimed at desegregating student enrollments and improving programs and facilities while retaining or enhancing their historic stature (OCR, 1991). This strategy closely resembles the purpose of the original system the HBCUs followed, when the initial goal was to provide for college-level programs and facilities for the otherwise disenfranchised black student. One should understand that before the Civil War, a comprehensive system of higher education was only just beginning to emerge and that opportunities for black participation in this system were few. In the early nineteenth century, in fact, it had been illegal in the Southern states to teach slaves to read or write (Morris, 1981). However, a transition in the national philosophy of black education emerged just prior to the Civil War and was solidified during the Reconstruction era, when black students were perceived as viable citizens entitled to educational opportunities. Under the auspices of the American Missionary Association and the Freedmen's Bureau, "Negro colleges" grew rapidly during Reconstruction (Anderson, 1988). Such schools were the pet projects of abolitionists and missionaries who came to the South with the expectation of organizing colleges open to all youth, designing and implementing schools that would teach poor students regardless of race.

Unfortunately, many perceived these schools as crossing racial boundaries in a presumptive manner. The transition from a non-segregated system to a segregated system, specifically the Negro college, is believed to be the result of local organizing dynamics purposed to disenfranchise African-Americans and embrace racial segregation. This action, of course, was not the result of the original intention of the founders of such schools, but HBCUs have since had to assume a significant role and responsibility for the intellectual development mainly of blacks.

From the beginning, HBCUs met the special needs of African-Americans who were usually less well prepared than their white counterparts. However, HBCUs in the modern era must meet educational objectives far beyond their modest initial goals of educational programs and facilities and, paradoxically, it is this new demand on the HBCUs that threatens their continued existence. The historical emergence of the demands of a desegregated educational environment is not a new occurrence, and this transition towards equitable education has been progressive throughout the structure and use of the HBCU. As late as 1914, black higher education was mostly private education (Jones and Richards-Smith, 1987).

The transition to public funding, especially in state-operated HBCUs, suggested, in effect, that the government itself sponsored and approved segregation. In fact, this governmental response remained generally accepted through the first half of the twentieth century but was thereafter subject to intense controversy.

In 1955, the Supreme Court ordered the desegregation of American schools with "all deliberate speed." But while the Court had determined that segregation was unconstitutional, it would not definitively address the detrimental effects, conditions and vestiges of segregation in regards to higher education until the 1990s. This inattention exerted a strong impact upon higher education in the HBCUs during the long years after *Brown,* for the local public school issues of mandatory busing, freedom of choice, zoning and residential gerrymandering remained irrelevant to higher education colleges and universities (Altbach, 1991). While segregation had been eliminated by court order at the lower levels, an undeniable *de facto* segregation persisted unaddressed in colleges and universities.

In the early stages of higher education desegregation, one finds a disproportionate shifting of black students to TWIs. As desegregation proceeded, the conviction among educators and judicial authorities grew that it was to flow in one direction, from black to white (Tollett, 1994). As state desegregation plans were developed under court orders and directives, they were at times, attended by calls for the closing of black institutions or their merger into white higher education. One estimate placed 82% of black students in colleges and universities in TWIs (Garibaldi, 1984).

Administrators of black institutions have, however, been slow to acknowledge this trend. Or, they assume that while the concept of affirmative action implies long-term objectives, ultimately they have served only in a temporary role at HBCUs in helping African-American students to catch up academically with white Americans. Few HBCU leaders, therefore, sought to broaden their institutional missions to appeal to a more general constituency (actively cultivating the enrollment of whites, Asians, Hispanics, American Indians and other racial and ethnic groups) for fear of alienating their mainly black constituency (Coleman, 1990). As a result, black institutions lost a lot of traditional enrollments to the now-open TWIs. This enrollment loss created financial distress that ultimately affected admissions, recruitment and retention, funding, program development and facilities. Today, declining student and faculty numbers, state budget cuts, unequal higher-education funding formulas, a troubled economy and negative institutional images complicate and fuel the debate over the viability of HBCUs.

It is essential to recognize that researchers have been studying HBCUs for more than 25 years; however, most of this research has focused on differences in admissions standards and graduation rates between HBCUs and TWIs. In general, most of the research falls into one of three types. First, some studies focus on admissions criteria and the differences between black and white qualifications. One need only examine the Supreme Court Cases of *Bakke* v. *Regents of California* (1978); *Hopwood* v. *University of Texas Law School* (1996); and in the *University of Michigan Law School case* (2003) in which flexible law admission standards incorporating "admission points" for racial minorities brought controversy centering on the issues of affirmative action, reverse discrimination and the extent an institution can go to achieve cultural diversity.

Second, some studies focus mainly on racial composition and degree completions between blacks and whites at TWIs or demographics and educational statistics related to graduation, retention, etc. (Roebuck, 1993). These studies provide relevant data on blacks at both HBCUs and TWIs but fall short in addressing a multitude of variables that may speak for the continued existence of an HBCU. If institutions only examine selective data without exploring the larger social, political and economical factors that influence this data, then much is missed or lost in truly understanding the experiences HBCUs offer.

Third, many studies focus on student achievement between race or ethnicity at HBCUs and TWIs (Wenglinsky, 1997). But justifying the continued existence of HBCUs requires more than discrete statistics. It involves satisfying the *Fordice* standard and determining how one proves that HBCUs provide an educational or sociological benefit or benefits in ways not provided by TWIs or at levels not nearly as great at TWIs.

Few studies have so far compared or even addressed the educational experiences and outcomes of students attending HBCUs and TWIs (Wenglinsky, 1997). Also, few studies have addressed the internal impact of desegregation as experienced by a specific institution. Even fewer studies have sought to explore the impact of Court desegregation rulings in terms of the subsequent responses of those who experienced it firsthand to inform and guide policymakers. An argument is being made that when research focuses on allowing institutions to share their views, their values and their experiences, that lessons can encourage the courts and legislative bodies to consider both short-term and long-term policies in defining and determining the roles and responsibilities of HBCUs.

These lessons tell us the good and the bad, what is plausible and what is non-applicable or non-practical in terms of academic achievement, student success, institutional effectiveness and supportive environments that ensure outcomes. Our nation's greatest resource is human capital. What is lacking in research on HBCUs is the exploration of studies that focus on institutions as viable solutions to their own dilemmas as projected through their own eyes and experiences. HBCUs are essentially put on a short leash and told what to do, how to do and with what to do. They are never allowed to participate as respectable contributing resources that can shed light into what works and what doesn't work in their given context or current existence. TWIs have a longer, larger leash to engage in far-reaching diverse efforts to contribute to society, conducting comprehensive research using technology, engaging in educational experiences with greater academic freedom and more flexible governance than HBCUs.

One sees the compelling need to study the impact of desegregation of HBCUs in light of *Fordice*. Accordingly, this study explored the current discussion and debate over the future of HBCUs. The empirical evidence generated by the research has not successfully identified any legal or educational justification that would be clear or permanently applicable for all HBCUs. But it is crucial to note that this might be because the right questions have thus far gone unexplored in the majority of the literature. For example, in the 1960s researchers were interested in discovering whether or not the occupational aspirations of black students were keeping pace with the new opportunities available to them. The most comprehensive study during this period found that HBCU students still tended to aspire to and enter low-status occupations; the study also found that women at HBCUs had lower occupational aspirations than their male counterparts (Gurin and Katz, 1966). That study had many limitations; however, the foremost being that it did not compare students attending HBCUs to students attending TWIs. Without such a comparison, it is impossible to know what benefits HBCUs provide that the TWIs did not. Indeed, later studies that have pointed to the social cohesion and educational outcomes at both HBCUs and TWIs have found the relationship between the two to be quite weak (Davis, 1991).

It is also interesting to note that black students who attend HBCUs were more likely to major in business, engineering or the sciences (Astin, 1996). This finding is significant from the perspective of the labor-market outcomes, because the income potential of these fields is higher than that of the liberal arts majors. Trent (1991) found black students attending HBCUs to be more likely to pursue non-traditional majors leading to professions historically denied to minorities. Thus, the value of HBCUs may lie in the educational choices, programs and support systems that they offer.

Federal History of Desegregation

The federal history of desegregation centers on the enforcement of the Fourteenth Amendment, which states that no U.S. citizens shall be denied equal protection under the law, nor be subjected to exclusion or discriminatory practices in programs that receive federal funds. Nonetheless, persons seeking educational equality have repeatedly had to put these lofty constitutional ideas to the test to determine whether they are rhetoric or reality. In case after case, many African-Americans have found the Constitution falling short of compelling the same protection for them as for whites (Medley, 1994).

In fact, the history of the Supreme Court's involvement with discrimination, race and desegregation—specifically in the context of public facilities, policy and educational institutions—reflects a long and intriguing record of inconsistent rulings and the nation's repeated failure to ensure equal rights for all Americans in general and African-Americans in particular.

In *Plessy* v. *Ferguson* (1896), the Court established the doctrine of separate but equal. This case pertained primarily to public accommodations; however, its impact was felt in the educational system because schools were set up separately for blacks and whites. Subsequent court cases such as *Siquel* v. *Oklahoma* (1948) and *McLauren v. Oklahoma* led to rulings admitting blacks to all white schools when black institutions did not offer comparable studies. Equally intriguing was that *Brown I* (1954) turned the tide of education on the elementary level as it struck down the doctrine of separate but equal, and *Brown II* (1955) forced the nation to integrate "with all deliberate speed." These cases dealt primarily with education prior to the collegiate level but set stage for higher education to evaluate its own purpose and existence in terms of race.

In 1978 *Bakke* v. *the Regents of California* reversed the gains of minorities in many ways because the ruling limited racial preferences in terms of admission on the secondary level. In later years, the nation witnessed race preferences in terms of admissions being overturned *(Hopwood* v. *Texas, 1996)*. The Court changed course again in 2003 when it ruled in the *University of Michigan Law School* case that racial preferences are permissible in higher education to ensure diversity and preparation of students to be able to work, socialize and live in a culturally diverse society.

The significance of these desegregation court cases is profound, for it appears that the desegregation efforts within the United States are mixed in terms of their overall successes. Some cases appear to constitute powerful desegregation efforts, and yet they are followed within a few years by qualifications and even reversals. Two questions remain elusive in the Court's rulings over the years: What has been the short and long term impact of desegregation on HBCUs. In the light of desegregation, what can be done to preserve their viability?

Policy Implications of Desegregation

Current Status of HBCUs

The answers to these two questions remain unclear, but HBCUs have undergone major changes recently. Changes in legislative and judicial requirements for state public higher education systems between 1954 and 1973 have resulted in a significant alteration of the demographics of HBCUs. For example, the opening of TWIs to black applicants has led to a decline in HBCU enrollments.

Currently, of the 103 HBCUs located in 19 states and within the District of Columbia, 53 are under private control and 50 are public institutions. Eighty-nine HBCUs are four-year institutions, and the rest are two-year institutions. Enrollments in all HBCUs range from under 1,000 to about 8,000 students, on average. In total, nearly 300,000 students now attend HBCUs (Hoffman, 1995). In response to the desegregation cases, HBCUs began to recruit white faculty members and students, although with less success than the TWIs had in recruiting blacks. By 1992, three HBCUs had become predominantly white, and 20 were more than 20% white. As of 1990, 13.1% of HBCU students were white, a 3.6% increase since 1976. Interestingly, HBCUs have also become increasingly "feminized," with the percentage of male students decreasing consistently from 47% in 1976 to 40.9% in 1990.

However, despite the increasing ethnic and gender diversity of these schools and the attraction of blacks to TWIs, HBCUs continue to educate large numbers of blacks. In fact, enrollment at HBCUs has recently begun to increase. Currently, 21% of all black postsecondary students attend HBCUs and 28% of all degrees awarded to blacks are from HBCUs. Finally, while enrollments remained constant from 1976 to 1986, there has since been a transition in enrollment with a 15% increase between 1986 and 1990.

It appears that as the demand for an HBCU education has begun to increase, government efforts to support the schools have declined. This is ironic, for it appears to go against the third determining point provided by the Supreme Court which is to prove that there is a separate, coherent demand for the HBCUs as opposed to single-strategy educational institutions. One reason is that reduced government support for the HBCU is found in the financial support issued at the state and the federal levels for these institutions. While total spending has increased at HBCUs, it does so at slower rates than at TWIs. In 1988-89 dollars, expenditures at HBCUs increased by 21.4% over the period 1976 to 1988, whereas the average increase for all universities was 26.6%. This failure to keep pace with other educational institutions created financial pressures on HBCUs. From 1986 to 1989, enrollments increased twice as quickly as revenues. Thus, resource problems have begun to re-emerge at HBCUs, only 30 years after the federal government singled them out as in need of financial (Hoffman et al., 1992).

The Plight of HBCUs

In addition to the current status of the HBCUs, both the historical and legal plight of HBCUs gave rise to serious policy challenges, implications and issues of major consideration by the courts, the states and the institutions themselves. All relevant cases prior to *Fordice* had considered K-12 mandatory education. In *Fordice*, for the first time, the Court had to decide what essential factors indicated unconstitutional segregation and what remedies applied. It is necessary at this point to reiterate that in its subsequent ruling in *U.S. v. Fordice*, the Supreme Court found four surviving aspects of Mississippi's *de jure* system constitutionally suspect (a) a reliance on minimum cut-off scores as the basis for admission standards, (b) program duplication, (c) disparate institutional mission assignments, and (d) inequitable institutional funding. The Court, in its 1992 decision in *U.S. v. Fordice*, further stipulated that Mississippi should eliminate policies that keep public colleges racially identifiable. However, institutions and state officials often disagree on how much emphasis should be placed on that objective. Most HBCU officials believe that they first need greater financing to offer the key quality academic programs and attractive campus attributes that will make the colleges more desirable to all students, including white students.

Beyond such factors, numerous faculty and staff members, students, alumni and administrators feel strongly that major policies have to address increasing educational opportunities for black people and that this should be accomplished, in part, by supporting and improving the only colleges that have historically provided them access to higher education. State officials agree on increases in money and program allocations as satisfactory policies; however, stipulations are often made on increasing white students to justify continued state aid. The goal of bringing more white students to black college campuses has itself been divisive within the HBCUs, enraging those students and college officials who don't understand why desegregation lawsuits originally lodged to protest unequal educational opportunities for black students are resolved in part by making black institutions more attractive and inclusive to white students as a means of justifying funding and, through this process, ensuring the continued existence of the HBCU (Hebel, 2001). Paradoxically, as of 2003, HBCUs nationwide remain predominantly black despite desegregation rulings and polices to make them more non-racially identifiable (Hebel, 2001).

Admissions Standards

Interestingly, HBCU admissions standards and decisions have historically been both challenging and controversial issues potentially influencing the very continuance of these institutions. On the one hand, the methods HBCUs use in admitting students have garnered success through creating environments that are more accepting to blacks than TWIs. On the other hand, their standards, arguably lower than those put in place by other academic institutions, have the potential to harm the HBCU through generating a substandard student pool. Within higher education, it is an accepted trait of all colleges and universities that there are articulated and implemented admissions criteria or standards that must be met by those seeking admissions to a given institution. These admissions criteria differ dramatically among institutions. For example, a student attempting to enroll at the University of Massachusetts at Lowell might be an exceptional candidate at this particular school but would be overlooked by many Ivy League institutions. This policy of admission standards is educationally sound if the underlying purposes of those standards are designed to ensure the social and intellectual development of discrete groups and types of learners. Observations are contingent on those said colleges and universities to keep a watchful eye on the impact of state policy on their admissions standards.

HBCUs have historically maintained lower and extremely flexible admissions criteria and, over the years of desegregation, these criteria and standards have evolved to both inclusion and exclusion of specific populations. Until recent years the courts have delegated the decision-making regarding corrective measures to address segregation in higher education to states. Among such routine and permissible factors for admission consideration are grade-point averages, class ranks, race, income, family background and other predictors of student success. But two other factors that are relevant to the selection of students within the HBCU must not be ignored, and these are:

1. Open admission policies. These policies do not discharge the affirmative duty imposed upon the state by the Constitution where, under policy,

there is no genuine progress toward desegregation and no genuine prospect of progress *(Sanders v. Ellington,* 1968, p. 937); and

2. When open admissions alone fail to integrate a segregated school system, be it a primary or secondary school system or a college system, then something more is required such as credit for unique life experience *(United States* v. *Louisiana,* 1988, p. 641).

In *Ayers* v. *Allain* (1987), a predecessor of the *Fordice* case, the Supreme Court ruled that freedom of choice was an acceptable policy: "As long as qualified students, black and white, can attend the type and quality of available institution they choose, there is no denial of equal protection" (p. 1523). In *United States* v. *Fordice,* the exclusive reliance of the Mississippi College Board on SAT and ACT scores for determining acceptance was deemed as having a disparate impact on minority students' admissions opportunities. Thus, according to the Supreme Court, it is apparent that opportunities under the Equal Protection clause of the Fourteenth Amendment were violated.

The nature of HBCU admission standards appears, therefore, to be a "catch-22" problem for these institutions, for while the student pool is broader and arguably more conducive to equality, the composite nature of this pool can be seen as potentially inferior to that of the TWI. This also has the awesome potential to negatively impact the HBCU through limiting its reputation, where a side-by-side comparison of those traits within the HBCU and the TWI in respect to admission standards might encourage the outsider evaluating the institutions on the basis of standards alone to perceive the HBCU as inferior. This, in turn, has the potential to negatively impact the student pool for the HBCU, creating a cyclical process wherein HBCUs fight against the connotation that they are inferior institutions. Surprisingly, few studies note this particular theme of conflict within the HBCU.

Program Duplication

In addition to the admissions challenges HBCUs face, the desire to survive as distinct institutions forces HBCUs to mount clear and distinct programs that warrant their necessity and survival. While this separation of programs did emerge in the past, it still remains true for the current HBCUs' survival.

Historically, HBCUs grew out of efforts to educate blacks without reference to whites and neither equality nor program duplication played any key roles in earlier efforts as programs were adopted. The principal intent of forming HBCUs acknowledged the futility of trying to educate the races together. But the modern day has created a new variety of challenges in terms of separating and promoting differing curricula and programs. For example, Mississippi state funding formulas favored TWIs under the pretense of those institutions offering full ranges of undergraduate, graduate and professional programs. Therefore, these TWIs should be classified as Research I-and Research II-level institutions and given priority in terms of funding and official attention, resources and support. HBCUs, conversely, have had to struggle to survive with lesser funding, a practice partially justified on the grounds that the TWIs offered the majority of necessary programs and therefore required the lion's share of funding. Indeed, the plaintiffs in *United States v. Fordice* made clear that the real issue was not program duplication but enhancement, where the funding provided to the HBCU was simply unequal to that offered regularly to Mississippi's TWIs and that this funding pattern promised to keep the HBCUs unequal.

Mission Assignments

Further complicating the existence and survival of HBCUs has been the attempt by political, educational and social forces over the last century to clearly define and dictate highly restrictive and specialized missions versus the comprehensive missions of TWIs. Historically, state governments have been casual about guiding and monitoring the development of HBCUs' missions. Due to the availability of generous resources, the traditionally white institutions could freely choose to become research institutions, midsize institutions or comprehensive institutions with a smorgasbord of professional schools. However, HBCUs have never had the kind of latitude that TWIs have had in the area of missions. In *United States v. Fordice,* the Court scrutinized Mississippi's classification scheme for institutional missions. Three of the predominantly white universities were classified as flagship institutions. They offered the most advanced programs, the broadest curriculums and therefore received by far the most funding in comparison to other institutions, specifically the HBCUs. HBCUs were limited in their mission to training teachers and providing training in the areas of agriculture and menial services. Consequently, their funding was limited.

Even in recent years as the missions of the HBCUs changed to reflect variations within society's social structures, their funding still reflected old policies based on *de jure* segregation. The issue at hand is that HBCUs have had to struggle to achieve the same state-imposed expectations and mission mandates with lesser and limited funding and resources. Equally clear is the fact that HBCUs historically have had clearly defined missions "to provide opportunities for higher education to those who have traditionally been denied such opportunities at majority institutions." But this mission, no longer clear, grows murkier by the semester.

Inequitable Funding *Vis-A-Vis* Equal Educational Opportunity

As the historically black colleges and universities have had clearly defined, restrictive and specialized missions, their existence and survival have been inextricably tied to funding limitations in their respective states. Historically, state legislative branches have distributed unequal funding allocations to address the existence and survival of HBCUs in terms of programs such as general revenue, expenditures, scholarships, facility financing, maintenance and general operating costs. However, as higher education faces diminishing funds and revenue shortfalls, the national economy grows progressively more uncertain and the generous backers of philanthropy move away from educational efforts, the question of financial sustainability within the HBCUs looms larger than ever.

Administrators and proponents of the HBCUs are forced to ask a series of questions designed to explore the scope of their institutions: (a) Will the problem of under-funding that currently plagues higher education prompt U.S. colleges and universities to limit enrollments, raise entrance standards, or impose selective admissions? (b) Will colleges and universities reduce those programs that help students overcome their academic deficits? (c) Will financial aid resources be depleted? (d) Will selected institutions be forced to merge or close? Answering *yes* to a single question or a combination of such daunting prospects confirms to some extent an erosion of equal opportunity afforded African-Americans in higher education. HBCUs have always had problems in securing sufficient funding to run their institutions. For public HBCUs, state funding, a source of revenue which has never been sufficient, is augmented by student tuition, grants and corporate and individual donations.

Inasmuch as state dollars have never been equal to or adequately balanced between TWIs and HBCUs, enhancement appropriations have often been tied to accountability measures such as enrollment, retention, graduation rates, excess course credit and research funding (Evans, 2002). In addition, the re-examination of higher education funding formulas in all of the former *de jure* segregation states is essential to the viability of the nation's HBCUs which, despite constricted resources, enroll and graduate significant numbers of ethnic minority students across the nation. The states must acknowledge the local value of HBCUs and their importance as national resources.

In light of all these challenges and obstacles, this study now examines how the State of Mississippi and its history of black education involving Jackson State University and the U.S Supreme Court interacted or crossed paths.

The State of Mississippi's Higher Education System

By 1992, there were at least 500 desegregation cases on file at the Department of Justice (Phillip, 1992). Currently, the political inclination to resolve tensions and eliminate segregation remains elusive. Thus, the courts maintain an indispensable role in the fight for equity and justice in postsecondary institutions. Practically impervious to massive transformations in the social and educational fabric of the United States over the last century, Mississippi retained its traditions of segregation, desegregation and pernicious legacy in higher education. HBCUs have continually redefined their respective purposes and missions. Consequently, this researcher undertook an analysis of the impact of desegregation on HBCUs and, notably on Jackson State University, in part by examining Mississippi's efforts to address, measure and support postsecondary education. This study addresses both the techniques and specific efforts utilized by the state towards its postsecondary institutions.

Accordingly, The Mississippi Institutions of Higher Learning (IHLMS), the governing body of the state's postsecondary institutions, historically and currently focuses on strategic themes and performance indicators to help students achieve their educational goals. These themes and indicators are broad-based and tend to focus on the system level. They serve as benchmarks in helping to assess postsecondary education efficiency and effectiveness. A benchmark is a set baseline, target value or performance indicator against which one can measure progress (Houten, 1996). In Mississippi, these themes and indicators serve as institutional effectiveness criteria that include quality, accessibility, affordability, accountability, economic development and diversity. The performance indicators occur in both the system and in the individual institutions and are therefore classified in those terms.

The troubled history of desegregation in Mississippi has perpetuated and left far-reaching implications and issues in both black and white institutions that continue to plague the progress of postsecondary education. Jackson State University, in particular, came into existence in response to the struggles and progress of Mississippi in providing its minority people with educational opportunities for success.

The History of Black Higher Education in Mississippi

Historically, the impact of segregation and the existence of postsecondary education in Mississippi can be seen as early as the 1800s. Prior to the Civil War, throughout the Confederacy and in Mississippi, educating black slaves was a crime. During Reconstruction, historically black colleges and universities were established by funds administered by the Freedmen's Bureau, limited funds under the 1862 Morrill Act for land grant colleges and by missionary and other charitable organizations. As noted previously, the early incarnation of these HBCUs was structured for all students regardless of race and focused on providing education predominantly for members of poorer communities.

However, Mississippi's five white colleges and universities at this time were designed and operated in accordance with a state-sanctioned *de jure* racial segregation scheme that limited the educational options for black students to the Reconstruction institutions. Indeed, the only HBCU opened in Mississippi in the nineteenth century was Alcorn State University (1871), an agricultural college specifically for Mississippi's black youth *(Allain* v. *Ayers 674* F. Supp. 1523 N.D. Miss. 1987).

Throughout the South, specifically Mississippi, HBCUs emerged as either the products of well-meaning Reconstructionists or were opened grudgingly by the state as a means of dodging similar Reconstruction initiatives. New HBCUs were opened and additional funds were appropriated for them only as a means of forestalling intervention by the federal government on behalf of black college students. Despite the opening of these schools, however, the HBCUs were consistently discriminated against in terms of funding, curriculum and admissions.

Consequently, many of the HBCUs were directed to curriculums of manual work, and overall these colleges were mandated as elementary schools, teaching trades and offering very little, if any, postsecondary coursework as their mission. The story of black education in Mississippi, as in so many other states, was the reflection of the typical attitudes of the "liberal white male Southerner." The freedmen might have schools and colleges, but education for black students would remain under-funded, unrecognized and relegated to second-class status. Graduates of these colleges could contribute in prescribed ways to the restoration of the South. They would not concern themselves with "rights" or pose a threat to white labor.

Northern philanthropists and missionary associations that came to Mississippi and other Southern states were not prohibited from developing private black colleges, so long as these institutions would accommodate the dominant/subordinate relationship between whites and blacks in the South.

It wasn't until the 1950s that there was a crack in the controlling constitutional legal authority established by the separate but equal doctrine established in *Plessy v. Ferguson,* as well as corresponding cases in the all deliberate speed section detailed previously. The impact of those decisions persuaded southern legislators to increase funding to the HBCUs, mainly as a method of lessening federal scrutiny. Consequently, scholarships at Southern HBCUs were increased on the average from 4 to 12% of the state regent's budget to permit few blacks to undertake graduate studies outside their respective states (O'Brien, 1999).

In addition, some HBCUs were upgraded to accredited four-year institutions that provided degrees, and created limited graduate faculties and departments. However, as a compensatory measure, admission requirements in TWIs overall and specifically in Mississippi were tightened in ways to screen out most blacks.

It is further noted that Mississippi's system of public four-year universities was segregated by race from its inception in 1848 until 1962, when the first black student was admitted to the University of Mississippi by court order. The racial identifiability of Mississippi's eight public universities changed little during the decade following the landmark admission of James Meredith. The student composition of Mississippi's eight postsecondary institutions remained almost entirely white, while its HBCUs—Jackson State University, Mississippi Valley State University and Alcorn State University—remained almost entirely black. Such occurrence among these institutions further did not reflect the state's population: 67% white and 33% black (Tate, 1999). It was a clear message to the public that Mississippi was far from representing equality and equal opportunity in terms of higher education. It is then understandable that an ensuing lawsuit about inequality between blacks and whites called *U.S. v. Fordice* would emerge a decade later to have a tremendous impact on Jackson State University.

Fordice: Mississippi and Desegregation Politics

As previously stated, Mississippi's eight postsecondary institutions held their distinctive racial identifiability as late as Fall 1996. The on-campus undergraduate enrollment ranged between 75% and 85% white at each of the TWIs and averaged nearly 98% black at each of the HBCUs. On the state level, the facts in the *Fordice* case are centered on Mississippi's efforts to continue a long-established policy of *de jure* segregation in its public-university system by maintaining "five almost completely white and three almost exclusively black universities" {*Fordice*, p. 2729). A group of private citizens, mostly African-

Americans, sued then-Governor Kirk Fordice of Mississippi for alleged racial discrimination within the state-university system.

Mississippi had a long-running history of denial and discrimination against people of color dating back before the Civil War, with limited reform in the period following. Blacks were not allowed to attend TWIs in Mississippi as late as 1962, a situation that was partially addressed when Medger Evers, a field secretary for the NAACP, sought to integrate the University of Mississippi. Prior to this time, blacks were denied access, admissions and assistance with higher education in TWIs and were forced to attend those HBCUs established by the Morrill Act of 1862. This act passed before the Emancipation Proclamation and provided federal funding and support but did not specifically address the educational needs of blacks.

Despite the focus of the second Morrill Act and similar legislation designed with the purpose of providing facilities towards minorities, the HBCUs were still not on par with the TWIs in the State of Mississippi. Unequal in instructional quality, funding, facilities, standards, resources and demographic access, Mississippi's HBCUs struggled against great disadvantages. Although the State of Mississippi had directly addressed dual systems of discrimination only at the elementary and secondary levels, the state could not deny or escape its obligation to dismantle the same discrimination imposed in higher education.

From the onset, the Court made clear its position in *United States* v. *Fordice* that Mississippi had not gone far enough to remedy past *de jure* discrimination practices, and it still had a constitutional obligation to dismantle its segregated programs. The primary issue before the Court was whether Mississippi had met an affirmative duty to dismantle its prior dual university system. Equally important, the Court also made clear that choice alone did not meet a state's duty to desegregate, thus reducing Mississippi's opportunities for cosmetic desegregation. These two criteria applied to Mississippi demonstrated to the justices of the Supreme Court that the state's legislative system was still participating in methods of sporadic and selective desegregation.

To further complicate the issue, the Mississippi system of higher education was unique in that the original 1975 lawsuit *(Ayers v. Fordice)* by the late Jake Ayers Sr. involved the father of a black college student who claimed that the State of Mississippi purposefully neglected historically black colleges and universities. Their argument was that the State of Mississippi had for decades under-funded its HBCUs. The plaintiff also argued that the state had not met the *Brown II* mandate to dismantle segregated education with all deliberate speed. They further charged that Mississippi's higher education system was in violation of the Fifth, Ninth, Thirteenth and Fourteenth Amendments to the United States Constitution (42 U.S.C. 1981 and 1983; and Title VI of the Civil

Rights Act of 1964, 42 U.S.C. 2000 to 2000d-4a). The United States intervened as plaintiff and alleged violations of the equal protection clause of the Fourteenth Amendment and Title VI. For 12 years the parties attempted to resolve their differences through a voluntary dismantling of the prior segregated system. Unable to achieve a mutual agreement, the parties proceeded to trial in 1987.

The respondents—the Board of Trustees of State Institutions of Higher Learning (the College Board)—maintained that the state had met the *Brown* mandate by adopting race-neutral policies. The U.S. District Court for the Northern District of Mississippi and the Fifth Circuit Court of Appeals applied their interpretation of the standard established in *Brown* and concluded that the state had met its affirmative duty to dismantle the former *de jure* segregated system of higher education with its adoption and implementation of good-faith, race-neutral policies and procedures in student admissions and other areas. The U.S. Supreme Court granted *certiorari*, then vacated the judgment and remanded for further proceedings, holding that the mere adoption and implementation of race-neutral policies were insufficient to demonstrate complete abandonment of the racially dual system. The Court noted:

> Even after a State dismantles its segregative admissions policy, there may still be state action that is traceable to the State's prior *de jure* segregation and that continues to foster segregation. If policies traceable to the *de jure* system are still in force and have discriminatory effects, those policies too must be reformed to the extent practicable and consistent with sound educational practices {*United States* v. *Fordice,* et. al 50 U.S. 120 L Ed. 2d 575).

The ruling of this case proved long before *United States* v. *Fordice* that Mississippi maintained a biased system of academic and educational performance. The Court held that Mississippi's TWIs required higher minimum admissions test scores than its HBCUs. Further, these institutions relied on standardized test scores (ACT and SAT) that inherently discriminated against blacks. Admission eligibility differed across the state and resulted in 72% of Mississippi's white high school seniors and 30% of black seniors being eligible for admission to Mississippi's TWIs.

Further troubling was the finding that 99% of Mississippi's white seniors attended its TWIs and 71% of Mississippi's black seniors attended the state's HBCUs. The dilemma was further complicated by the reality of the element of free choice, unlike that of forced integration with the state's compulsory education. The Court could not force postsecondary education integration nor could it escape the controversy over the issues of free choice, quotas and reverse discrimination regarding admissions.

Despite Mississippi's changes in admissions policies and criteria, the U.S. Supreme Court ruled in 1992 that the state still had segregated universities. In March 1995, U.S. District Court Judge Neal Biggers Jr. ruled that the state was continuously perpetuating the vestiges of *de jure* segregation in the areas of undergraduate admissions, institutional mission assignments, funding, equipment deployment, library allocations, program duplication, land-grant programs and number of universities. Judge Biggers further ordered the state to spend more money to improve its HBCUs. First, "diversity scholarships" were to be funded to attract white students, and HBCUs and their respective campuses were required to appear less "black."

In 1997 and 1998, each HBCU was to spend approximately $150,000 on other-race diversity scholarships. In essence, white students now became the "minority" at HBCUs. Second, graduate programs would be added at Alcorn State University and Jackson State University. For Alcorn State University, the judge ordered Mississippi to create a $5 million endowment as well as matching grants of up to $4 million to enhance the institution. In addition, an MBA program was created at Alcorn's off-campus center in Natchez. For Jackson State University, the judge ordered the state to spend $20 million to establish an endowment and new programs in the fields of allied health (e.g. medical assistant), social work, urban planning and business. All of these programs were approved and funded by the Mississippi State Board of Trustees. At historically black Mississippi Valley State University, the state decided on its own to add graduate degree programs in the areas of elementary education and criminal justice (Fletcher, 2001).

Even before these financial incentives began, the *Fordice* decision ignited controversy because it stipulated a strict set of standards to be used by state legislatures and its subsidiary bodies in determining an educational justification for the continuance of HBCUs. The Court did not say how to sustain the HBCUs but left it for the state to decide. Mississippi's state legislature was now required to eliminate single-race institutions unless there is a compelling legal and/or educational justification for their existence. *Fordice,* in short, sent clear messages and several unclear messages.

Fordice essentially said that any consideration of HBCU continuance has to stipulate its three-tier standard. Any and all other previous discussions bear little, if not limited, input on HBCUs and their future. It further conveyed the idea that if a state could not reach the Court's standard, it could terminate the HBCU. This alternative obviously placed the future of many HBCUs in jeopardy. What was missed by many citizens was the reality that the state could end up consolidating or merging most HBCUs and have only one remaining. Or, it was possible for the state to have an HBCU merge with a TWI and the traditions of black heritage and culture become housed in museums rather than existing continually as society evolves.

On the other hand, *Fordice* further gave retribution in terms of millions of dollars to many HBCUs for years of discrimination by the State of Mississippi. But *Fordice* also established a hurdle that may be impossible to surmount by an HBCU. In order for an HBCU to continue to exist, it has some initial options. HBCUs can have their missions redefined in ways that may or may not include their previous historical roles and responsibilities. The other option is that HBCUs have to do things that are not done at TWIs or they have do whatever they are doing now exceptionally well, which is graduating minorities in specific fields at high rates or even higher rates than TWIs. One would have thought that *Fordice* was an absolute answer to a prayer. Many African-American citizens of Mississippi heralded the decision in *Fordice* as a major victory.

Others, such as Dr. James D. Anderson (1999), Professor of Education at the University of Illinois and leading authority on black education, compared the rulings in the case to "band-aids put on cancer." Dr. Anderson argued that the evidence brought before the Court to demonstrate the existence of discrimination and inequality was as persuasive "as you'll ever get." According to Anderson, the people involved in rectifying the situation were able to look at 130 years of Jim Crow and its negativity on education, then address the negative impact with a "token remedy" and "just move on." Dr. Anderson believed that the Court-ordered responses were like "grains of sand on a beach of what was needed to be done" (Anderson, 2001).

In addition to these initial rulings, other remedies in addition to white minority scholarships were subsequently made to address the *de jure* segregation in Mississippi higher education. Judge Biggers stopped short of ordering the closing of Mississippi Valley State University (MVSU), whose enrollment is overwhelmingly black, and merging it with predominantly white Delta State University (DSU) as the state had proposed. The Court issued an order for the Board of Trustees to undertake further study of "any educationally sound alternatives" to consolidation of the two schools.

There became a clear disagreement within Mississippi's educational community regarding the closings and mergers of schools. On one hand, pressure grew to expand the current system by creating university "satellite centers" via HBCUs throughout the state to primarily address full-time working residents. On the other hand, others argued that the satellite centers are not necessary and that some of the eight universities (inclusive of HBCUs) should be closed, merged or consolidated.

Furthermore, *Fordice* forced Mississippi to re-evaluate increasing HBCU admission standards since the Court mandated the same admission standards on all of Mississippi's institutions of higher education. Such a controversial move brought contention between blacks and whites. Under Judge Biggers' decision, high school graduates with at least a 3.2 GPA could gain automatic admission to any of Mississippi's eight universities. Those with at least a 2.5 GPA needed to score 16 or higher on the ACT. Students with a 2.0 GPA needed to score 18 or higher on the ACT.

These demarcations proved sensitive and problematic because of the fall-out. The new higher admission standards could possibly cause freshman enrollment to drop 50% at Jackson State, Mississippi Valley State and Alcorn State Universities from 1996 and afterwards. Such a move could also put black schools behind several years and put minority students at greater risk. Proponents, on the other hand, saw the new admission standards as an effective and immediate means to rid the state of one of the vestiges of segregation—the differential admissions requirements identified by the Court—as well as an opportunity to align Mississippi's universities with national and regional trends toward higher education.

This hope for equality within higher education was not unique to Mississippi, but it actually established an unusual situation in which three major state systems of higher education—those of Mississippi, Louisiana and Alabama—would be impacted simultaneously. In April 1997, the U.S. Court of Appeals for the Fifth Circuit ruled on an appeal of Judge Biggers' March 1995 ruling. The Court eventually defined specific target areas for which reforms directed towards a more comprehensive state of racial equality would have to be addressed (in such matters as admissions, missions, funding and program allocations) to ensure equal protection and provisions for both historically black and white institutions of higher learning. These three states were selected for reform as federal judges in the states of Mississippi, Louisiana and Alabama found their respective public higher education systems to be illegally segregated and attributed this continuing segregation to historical vestiges of segregation (Jaschik, 1995).

The Supreme Court maintained in its ruling that the higher education system of Mississippi would serve as the model for other state higher education systems in question. An additional point of concern in the *United States* v. *Fordice*, was that many district cases in Mississippi were on appeal before the Supreme Court for the purposes of defining the scope and relevance of the decision case. Thus, the *Fordice* precedent enabled state and lower federal courts to deal with segregated higher educational institutions in Mississippi and elsewhere.

While the intent of the Court was to create educational equity in higher education, the standards set forth in the *Fordice* decision for the racial integration of Mississippi's colleges and universities potentially jeopardized the constitutional standing and possible future existence of many HBCUs. The decision had the effect of suggesting that the HBCU was arguably inherently unnecessary once comparable education was equally provided to all students.

In essence, the *United States* v. *Fordice* decision raised more questions than it answered because after 26 years of litigation on the federal level, the State of Mississippi reached accord in its desegregation case. In 2002, a $502 million settlement was reached between the U.S. Department of Justice and Mississippi's Board of Trustees of State Institutions of Higher Education. This settlement was intended to address decades of deliberate racial segregation in its state colleges and universities.

The agreement seeks to improve academic programs and facilities at the state's historically black universities—Jackson State, Alcorn State and Mississippi Valley State Universities in particular—for the next 17 years. However, what the settlement does not answer or address is the overall impact of desegregation on Jackson State University in particular, in terms of its institutional effectiveness and clearly defined its future role in the State of Mississippi. Further, the court left intact the necessity for affirmative action, yet it noted that as of 2001, those affirmative policies have had questionable effects in diversifying and equalizing Mississippi's higher education system, and the state had not gone far enough to resolve it.

Jackson State University and its Relationship to *Fordice*

In Mississippi, a new urban college, Jackson State University, was established in 1940 solely to train "black teachers for black schools" *{United States* v. *Fordice,* 1992). This institution was considered unique on several fronts because it would emerge as the black flagship university because of its urban location, extensive black population and political relations with the State of Mississippi. Jackson State University soon attracted the largest concentration of African-American students to the most qualitative and quantitative programs offered by an HBCU in Mississippi, and it provided by far the greatest number of African-American faculty members.

Since its inception, Jackson State University has received the most meager allocations of state funds, a situation tied to the ancient racist attitudes and ideologies of Mississippi legislators and higher education officials from the prior segregated system. From the start, Jackson State was considered second-class compared to almost any TWI in Mississippi in terms of its admissions, curriculum, mission practices and program allocations.

This dilemma, which centered on Jackson State University, emerged and resulted in *United States* v. *Fordice* and is clearly detailed within this study: On the one hand, Jackson State University sought to preserve its historical role and existence while, on the other hand, it was challenged through the desegregation of TWIs within Mississippi. Jackson State University found itself in a position where it had to address both challenges without allowing itself to be eliminated, minimized or redefined in terms of its past mission. And it had to meet all these disparate challenges amid ambivalence in black institutions to provide education and training that would adequately serve the specific needs of blacks in society. In short, Jackson State University was forced, like so many other HBCUs, first to recognize and then to remain true to the realization that its major function was to prepare *all* of its students to meet their aspirations while it reached several benchmarks toward this goal by helping its black students meet the social, cultural, and racial challenges modern society presented.

Like all other HBCUs, Jackson State University finally concluded that one of its primary justifiable reasons for existence and continuation after *Fordice* was the need to help its newly diverse student body face and meet these social challenges. Indeed, one can argue that the educational process for blacks cannot be divorced from the dominant political, social and economic forces active in society and that the HBCU is the institution that best meets these goals (Lemelle, 2002).

CHAPTER THREE

Methodology of the Study

This chapter sets forth the methods of research employed. A descriptive case study is used to address the research question(s) pertaining to the desegregation impact on Jackson State University. The original research questions were: (a) What evidence exists to justify the continued existence of HBCUs for the twenty-first century? (b) What has been the impact of desegregation on one particular HBCU, Jackson State University, in terms of institutional effectiveness relating to key performance indicators? (c) Are HBCUs continuing to fulfill an unique role and addressing the needs of African-Americans? (d) What are the internal perceptions of Jackson State University regarding the impact of desegregation?

There are several reasons for employing the descriptive case-study methodology for this study. Case studies are designed to answer the "how and why" questions regarding a particular phenomenon and are appropriate for "situations where it is impossible to separate the phenomenon's variables from their context." Thus case studies "concentrate on many, if not all, the variables present in a single unit" (Merriam 1988). When a bounded system (i.e., program, process, institution or social group) has been identified as the focus for investigation and all the above apply (i.e., concern regarding analytic generalizations, concentration on numerous or all variables and concern with answers to how and why questions), then the case study provides an appropriate methodology.

Because case studies are particularistic (i.e., focused on a particular event, issue or phenomenon) and are by nature descriptive (i.e., providing the opportunity for thick description of the phenomenon under study), they offer the opportunity for a whole appreciation of a phenomenon within its natural context. Equally important is that a descriptive case study will allow for an optimum exploration into how and why various factors have caused a certain type of impact on the organization in question.

The descriptive case study can analyze the specific and unique impact of the desegregation court ruling and provide opportunities to measure the institutional effectiveness of Jackson State University mandated by the State of Mississippi's Council on Higher Learning. This method also allows for an analysis of the desegregation impact and the perceptions of those who experienced the impact firsthand. The descriptive case study allowed the investigator to identify quantitative data such as headcounts, enrollment trends, mission assignments, graduation rates and instructional programs offered. This method also allowed the investigator to explore and ascertain qualitative data in the form of interviews to address the research questions. The interviews were used to allow for the recording and analysis of perceptions by those key administrators who implemented policies and were held accountable for institutional effectiveness both to the state legislature (i.e., the Council on Higher Learning) and to the students of Mississippi who attended Jackson State University. Such findings helped to provide a thorough understanding of whether or not there was justifiable evidence for either the continuance or discontinuance of Jackson State University as an HBCU in Mississippi.

The methodology used allows this study to achieve prescriptive results which can then be used in clearly defining and determining the viability of Jackson State University for the twenty-first century.

Description of Data Sources

The methodology chapter is divided into three sections. First, a discussion of the organizational structure model used in this study is provided to contribute a rationale for selecting the subjects interviewed. This model was created from information gathered from Jackson State University's accreditation report published in 2002. Further, the analysis and results of the organizational structure of Jackson State University are used to depict the hierarchy of institutional leadership charged with implementing and accounting for the court-ordered desegregation policies and objectives. The individuals in the hierarchy who make up the leadership of Jackson State University are identified as "gatekeepers." A written explanation is provided to define these gatekeepers, their role and their relationship to the institution's hierarchy of leadership.

The second section discusses quantitative data on Jackson State University as compared to TWIs in Mississippi from both system-wide and institutional core indicators. A compare and contrast basis is provided with this quantitative data which was obtained from published reports, articles and books, archival records, institutional self-study reports and accreditation reports from the

Council on Higher Learning in Mississippi (the state's oversight commission for postsecondary education) and SACs (Southern Association of Colleges and Schools). This information is given context through tables with accompanying interpretations, summary analyses and identification of sources.

The third section discusses qualitative data in which administrative individuals in leadership roles, gatekeepers, are interviewed. The qualitative data, interview questions, were derived from the quantitative data, explored and examined by the researcher. Subsequently, the interview discussions were used to answer and respond in general to the initial research questions posed in Chapter One.

Throughout the recording of the qualitative interview data, direct quotes and summary comments from the gatekeepers of the institution are provided to reflect their personal feelings, thoughts and experiences with the desegregation process. Further, the qualitative data includes narrative discussion that conveys the personal expectations and experiences of this researcher in interacting with the institution as the data was collected. A brief discussion of the limitations of the study is included.

Leadership Organizational Structure

The Gatekeepers

Higher education leadership has many facets. Some institutions are characterized with total quality management involving significant and ongoing input from top to bottom and from bottom to top. Other institutions are primarily faculty-driven, where faculty are the key power brokers heavily influencing the decisions and directions of the institution. Yet other institutions are administrator-driven. The administrators initiate and finalize the course of direction and the day-to-day mechanics of the institutions. In many cases, some faculty and far more students have little or no input or significant influence on the ultimate decisions that are made. Institutional effectiveness is determined by many issues, many factors and many variables (LaRouche, 1976).

To fully understand Jackson State University's ability to be institutionally effective and to address the needs of its constituents, it became necessary to use the case study methodology to allow an internal look at the organizational structure, or model, used by the institution's leadership. The organizational structure in place at Jackson State University reflected the institution from a leadership perspective that identified which key players or decision-makers are effectuating day-to-day operations and progress.

I sought to obtain this information by examining the institution's own published organizational structure from its admissions catalog, self-study documents and accreditation reports. The organizational structure of Jackson State University depicts the president serving as the chief academic officer of the institution, supported by various senior-to entry-level administrators (vice-provosts, vice-presidents, deans, directors, chairs, specialists and support staff). Jackson State University is primarily administrator-driven by individuals who hold major administrative positions and roles. The faculty has significant input, but overwhelming the administration dictates the directions in which things flow at Jackson State University.

The gatekeepers were chosen because they represent a combination of administrators, a few faculty members and some staff persons who operate both as individual administrative leaders and committee members with delegated assignments ensuring institutional effectiveness through the Curriculum, Faculty and Staff Development, and the Admissions and Student Retention Committees, etc. In addition, these leaders serve in the essential offices of Institutional Research, Academic Affairs, Finance and Student Affairs.

Among their multiple duties are the roles and responsibilities of assessment and evaluation, planning and accountability reporting to the president of Jackson State University. Through this process, they ultimately provide institutional effectiveness reports to the Mississippi Council on Higher Learning. Further, they function as part of a practical process impacting how administrators make decisions, interpret information, apply policies, implement strategies and perpetuate accountability to both the Council on Higher Learning and its constituents (the students), whom it serves on a daily basis.

Although a lot of research is composed of surveys and input from faculty and students, this study focused on the primary input from administrators because they serve as the chief negotiators and bargaining agents among the institution, its constituencies and the State's Council on Higher Learning in terms of desegregation polices, practices and procedures. In these particular roles, they have access and perceptions that enable them to see and influence upfront the politics, power plays, policies and programs that relate to the institution.

The administrative support staff were also interviewed because they experience both external and internal factors that influence relationships, decisions and directions in which the institution goes through their service to the state, the top institutional leadership, the faculty, the student body and the general public. It was my belief that they could offer vivid and valuable insights and unlimited perspectives on Jackson State University's desegregation experiences in light of *Fordice* because they have handled policies, procedures and practices while providing essential progress reports to reporting authorities and public agencies.

Consequently, these senior administrators, junior administrators and some entry-level administrators were interviewed regarding data findings as well as their own perceptions of Jackson State University in terms of policies, practices, student success, campus atmosphere and the institution's own public image and mission through the pre-and post-desegregation litigation. By conducting a qualitative open-ended exploratory study, it was possible to revise the model as other significant factors emerged from the data.

The organizational structure researched in this study reflected a wide range of leaders and staff members in positions with diversified roles and responsibilities. Their goals are, of course, to carry out the leadership objectives of the president and to fulfill the institution's mission as mandated by the Mississippi State Legislature and overseen by the Council on Higher Learning. What is also clear is the existence of senior-level administrators, mid-level administrators and entry-level administrators who primarily serve as front-line soldiers addressing the needs of the institution. These gatekeepers protect, provide and perpetuate the president's vision, direction, and directives and respond to the needs of the institution's constituents. At this point, I wish to make clear that not all individuals listed as gatekeepers are necessarily completely supportive and in agreement with the president's vision, leadership and direction. Nor should the reader assume that any person identified as an "interviewee" is completely knowledgeable of the policies, dynamics and political factors that influence action or institutional effectiveness. Nor should the reader assume that all gatekeepers literally interact, understand and address issues directly or routinely with Mississippi's Council on Higher Learning.

The administration has the final and ultimate authority of submitting to the legal, political and policy decisions of the state's postsecondary education oversight commission (the Council on Higher Learning). The administration also ultimately enforces court rulings and legislative policies (via the Council on Higher Learning) through which the institution fulfills its mission of higher learning and education.

Administration as defined here includes the president and chief academic officers that carry out the mission, the mandates and the council's policies for the institution. These parties have the greatest influence as to what is accepted and rejected via curricula, student retention, academic programs and services provided to ensure student success. Through the process of soliciting and receiving information, recommendations and feedback, the administrators supervise the faculty and staff who provide learning experiences for the students and the general public which receives services. These gatekeepers are also the "pulse" or the "temperature" of the institution in terms of overall academic quality of learning, student success and satisfaction, employee morale and social perceptions as well as the practical effects of policies implemented, directed and ordered by the Council on Higher Learning, the Mississippi State Legislature and the Court.

The Mississippi Board of Trustees of State Institutions of Higher Learning

Equally relevant and important in understanding the impact of desegregation on HBCUs, particularly Jackson State University, are the existence, role and relationship of the Council on Higher Learning in Mississippi to the institution. The Mississippi State Institutions of Higher Learning, often referred to as the Council on Higher Learning, is the constitutional body of 12 board members that are appointed by the sitting governor and approved by the state legislature. Essentially, this body is responsible for policy and financial oversight of the eight public institutions of higher learning. Their duties range from addressing issues, concerns, policies, procedures and practices with each of the institutions in the areas of finance, administration, public affairs, development, technology, planning and budget, and judicial orders from the Supreme Court of Mississippi. On a day-to-day basis, they are also responsible for carrying out the state's constitutional responsibilities and accessible educational opportunities for all Mississippians regardless of race, color and gender.

Further, this Council works closely with each of the postsecondary educational institutions' executive officers (or college presidents) and institutional administrators, state and government officials, the education community, businesspersons and the public in increasing access to public higher education.

They are of particular significance in this study of desegregation in Mississippi because it is the Council's duty to engage in oversight of Jackson State University for it to achieve institutional effectiveness and address the needs of its constituents. This same Council also oversees the two other smaller and less-comprehensive HBCUs, Mississippi Valley State University and Alcorn State University.

The Council primarily works week to week throughout the year to ensure accurate and accountable statistical reporting that reflects enrollment trends, degree completions, institutional funding, graduation rates, student retention and instructional programs. On one hand, one can see the Council as the entity that ensures Mississippi is getting the best return on its dollars invested in both the institutions and the individuals who seek a public higher education. Equally important is that they frequently exist as the personal contact or liaison between the state legislature and the higher education institution. This liaison relationship has been historically strained, complicated and tenuous at best, because the Council on Higher Learning's existence and role have been historically interwoven with accusations that it both possesses and perpetuates vestiges of racism in dealing with HBCUs in Mississippi. Their role and responsibilities are further complicated because they oversee Jackson State University and hold it accountable but cannot completely address any and all the needs of Jackson State University because the institution has semi-autonomy. In lay terms, the Council is the "middle man" with essentially no middle ground to please all interested parties in achieving their respective legislative objectives and institutional goals. To do such, it runs the risk of damaging public trust, causing irreparable communication damage and creating friction between itself and the institution in question.

I interviewed three key administrative policy makers from the Mississippi Council on Higher Learning who explained and elaborated on their respective roles, responsibilities and the relationships among the Council and the eight postsecondary institutions in Mississippi.

The Data Collection Process

Quantitative and Qualitative Data

With this background and perspective in mind, it is necessary now to discuss the data collection process used for this dissertation. The data were collected over a period of 6 months from December 1, 2002 until May 31, 2003. Information on enrollment trends and characteristics as a whole was obtained from Mississippi's Council on Higher Learning Annual Report (2002), an edition that provides cross-comparative admission enrollment headcounts and graduation rates data on graduates from all higher education institutions (HBCUs and TWIs) in the state. Additional information was obtained through official written requests and interview sessions with three higher education administrators at the Mississippi Council on Higher Learning.

The information reported from these respective offices provides specific data including institutional cross-comparative data pertaining to degree completions, curricula and instructional programs offered and mission statements. These specific data were then classified and labeled as "performance indicators" in measuring institutional effectiveness at Jackson State University.

Two purposes were achieved with this action: First, it allowed this researcher to cross-compare Jackson State University with TWIs in Mississippi on state-required measurable outcomes within a quantitative context; second, it allowed exploring internal views and perceptions of administrators and a few faculty members within Jackson State University relative to the impact of desegregation, using the data and relevant questions about the data as a basis for discussion.

Interview questions were formulated based on thorough reviews of the published literature and annual reports from the Mississippi Council on Higher Learning. Additional data were ascertained via official written correspondence to the Office of Institutional Research. The response to these numerous requests generated institutional data inclusive of: (a) Jackson State University's self-study, and (b) excerpts from the institution's most recent Southern Association of Colleges and Schools (SACS) Accreditation Report. Essential data relevant to the interests and concerns of this researcher were further requested by official written and oral (telephone) requests to the Office of the President for access to resources and personnel on campus. Specifically, the president was asked for administrative permission to interview key administrative personnel and staff at the institution. The following personnel were allowed permission to be interviewed:

1. Chief of Staff,

2. Vice-Provost of Student Life and Related Staff,

3. Director of Institutional Research and Staff,

4. Office of Auxiliary Services,

5. Academic Admissions/Record/Support Staff, and

6. Director of Student Services.

The chief of staff serves as the administrative right hand to the president. After I made initial telephone contact with the chief of staff, she discussed with me the nature and purpose of this dissertation. She generously offered her time, insight and assistance in helping me to strategically identify key essential personnel who would best serve as gatekeepers or decision-making leaders of the institution. These initial senior-to entry-level administrators and staff were identified as individuals directly in touch with the desegregation issues involving Jackson State University.

Through the process of emails and direct phone contact by the chief of staff of Jackson State University's employees, this researcher was able to contact and arrange appointments with the personnel identified as gatekeepers. All of the gatekeepers had been previously informed by the chief of staff of this dissertation's purpose and the necessity for the interviews. These first individuals contacted were identified as executive-level administrators. Jackson State

University has five officials who serve in provost rankings with acting, assistant and associate designations. Many of their staff members contacted were receptive and responsive to this researcher's request to interview them and have their views shared from personal perspectives. In addition, these initial gatekeepers provided referrals to key mid-level and entry-level personnel who could provide additional insights, information and input on the desegregation impact experienced by Jackson State University. This researcher's request for data classified as "social perceptions" gave rise to the actual interviews taking place between March 1, 2003 and June 1,2003.

Interviews

An interview has been called a "conversation with a purpose" (Burgess, 1992). It is the major data collection strategy when a human investigator serves as the instrument in the collection and analysis of data. Naturalistic inquiry usually begins with interviews that are fairly open-ended and unstructured becoming more structured and focused during the latter stages of the research project (Merriam, 1988). Unstructured interviews, however, are fairly demanding and stressful. The interviewer must at once listen, keep track of the research protocol, reflect, interpret, sort themes, take notes and pace the overall interview appropriately.

During the course of the interview data collection process, notes were taken and expanded soon after the interview was conducted. Interviews were begun with "grand tour," open, non-directive questions that provide opportunity for the respondent to warm up to the interviewer, for trust to develop between the respondent and the interviewer and for the natural language and categories specific to the situation and/or the respondent's perspectives to emerge. Themes emerged spontaneously from the warm-up phase of the interview, and those same themes that were relevant to the problems or issues were then reflected back to the informant for further elaboration. Subsequently, specific detailed questions were asked and explored.

As the interview data collection process evolved, the story of Jackson State University's desegregation experiences came increasingly into focus. The interviews became semi-structured and, at times structured with specific questions tailored for eliciting information to help fill in gaps and address any discrepancies. Although the majority of the interviews were pre-arranged and carried out with prepared interview protocols and adequate information on the interviewee, a number of impromptu informal discussions yielded serendipitous insights.

Interviews were conducted with the chief ranking administrative officers and personnel who oversee day-to-day operations in their respective areas.

These employees range in ranking from entry-level to senior-level positions and constituted the study's interview pool. All interviewees were asked the same general questions about the institution's image, missions and goals, etc. Also, they were allowed an opportunity to offer and discuss issues and subjects they personally deemed relevant. A total of 25 persons were interviewed, in the following composition:

1. Executive-level administrators (5),
2. Mid-level directors (5),
3. Institutional specialists (5),
4. Administrative staff (5), and
5. Entry-level and related service-oriented position holders (5).

This researcher was aware of his own bias and qualifications in conducting a study that including his prior HBCU undergraduate education and social experience. The researcher's background (a master's degree in psychology and clinical experience) also influenced the interview approach and selection of interviewees.

Interviews were conducted by phone and summarized through oral and written communication. The length of the interviews was, on average, between 30 and 45 minutes with all parties interviewed separately. Follow-up interviews occurred on the average of two to three additional times per interviewee. This researcher was able to obtain detailed comments, concerns and answers when needed. All individuals were asked the same general questions pertaining to the institution's mission, social climate and views about desegregation experiences a second time to ensure clarity in what was asked in terms of their personal perceptions. Some respondents did not answer, or were unable to answer, some of the questions because the questions did not directly relate to their duties or they were not completely knowledgeable as to answers.

Only five interviews were recorded due to technical problems. The vast majority of the data obtained through the interviews via telephone was documented by this researcher via note-taking. To compensate for any discrepancies, all interviewees were forwarded a written copy of the interview questions with a summary analysis of the discussion and commentary to accommodate additional responses for clarification, corrections or adjustments, etc. The interviewees were thanked in writing by this researcher, asked to verify the accuracy of the information they provided and add any additional thoughts not originally discussed via telephone that they felt was vital. Interviewees were then asked to return the acknowledgement statements to this researcher's address. Their comments and direct quotes are included in the written study.

Data Summary

Finally, the quantitative data, consisting of reports, tables and relevant information, were contextualized with interpretations and summary analyses. The qualitative data were summarized. Based on their own perceptions of the desegregation experience and impact, the various interviewee positions regarding the continued existence and role of Jackson State University were then charted and categorized in the following contexts:

Table 3.1
Jackson State University's Role and Existenc

Gatekeepers' Opinions		
Support (Integrationists)	Do Not Support (Anti-Integrationists)	Undecided/Uncommitted (Neutralists)
These individuals basically support the existence of JSU as non-racially identifiable but not exclusively denying its black historical Heritage.	These individuals do not readily support the current leadership direction of JSU becoming non-racially identifiable. This group seeks to retain and perpetuate a historical and future black dominant culture on campus with little or no reception for the inclusion of whites into the mainstream affairs of JSU.	These individuals do not vocally or visibly take a stand supporting JSU as a non-racially or racially identifiable institution. They view themselves as important and relevant, but powerless, with no means to significantly affect change that will offer them security.

Limitations of the Study

Despite the acquisition of both relevant quantitative data and qualitative data, this study has several limitations. First, the findings may not universally apply to every HBCU as each has its own unique and distinct history, problems, political influences, challenges and obstacles that it has had to overcome. The experiences of HBCUs are common, yet varied and distinctly different one from another. What applies at one HBCU to enable its continuance or discontinuance does not necessarily apply to the continuance or discontinuance of others. experiences that support or impinge on their abilities to receive a higher education in Mississippi. Students fail and/or do not complete their studies, degrees and programs for different reasons that may be within the sphere of institutional influence or well beyond its control such as family dynamics and support systems, residence and personal challenges, etc.

This, study also does not tell every key experience of each administrator, faculty member, student or citizen of Mississippi who has attended Jackson State University and been impacted by its desegregation. The persons interviewed are the front-line enforcers of state and institutional policies directly responsible for oversight, insight and institutional reporting internally and externally through the respective chains of command stipulated by the Mississippi Council on Higher Learning and the institution. Very few faculty members and students were interviewed because of their lack of availability; their transient, semester-to-semester nature; and their limited direct roles and access to direct influence on policy decisions.

Another limitation of this study is its inability to fully explain several major factors occurring between 1975 and 2002 that had critical impact on the effectiveness of Jackson State University, such as funding, financial aid and student support systems.

This study was also limited by its duration and location. Information was gathered over one time period or decade, depending on the specific type of data needed. Some records no longer existed. More records were not accessible. Further, to understand an HBCU and, particularly Jackson State University, one needs to look at the institution's origin, history, experiences and future plans on a continuum (and not just on an historical basis) to determine how its survival can be best sustained.

Other limitations of this study are: (a) Major community issues such as race, politics, socialization and the background of all the students served through this institution are ignored or not wholly entertained; (b) The nature or degree of desegregation from the perspectives of many past and current students was not taken into account; (c) The question of why and to what extent historically white universities in Mississippi must be desegregated while HBCUs must be increasingly integrated with more whites was not addressed; (d) The latitude Jackson State University will have in utilizing increased funding resources from the State of Mississippi's recent desegregation ending was not investigated; (e) The extent to which Jackson State University can politically, socially and economically control its existence and future role exclusively was not determined, because such factors and variables change literally week to week, month to month, year to year and legislative tenures to legislative tenures.

CHAPTER FOUR

Descriptive Data

This study sought to give two descriptive views of Jackson State University for the reader to gain a thorough grasp on the desegregation experience at this institution. In this section called "Results of the Data Findings," the reader is exposed to concrete quantitative data. Much of the data presented from 1975-2002 was limited because various council reporting offices maintained only relevant yearly statistics and reports on an as-needed basis and were not readily accessible. Nevertheless, data is still presented to give an initial comprehensive view of Mississippi public higher education in terms of overall system and institution core indicators. A cross-comparative approach using tables and summary analyses is used to interpret data from the state's eight public higher education institutions.

These initial indicators primarily relate to quality, affordability, accessibility, economics, efficiency and diversity among the state's public institutions. Afterwards, key selected performance indicators at Jackson State University are addressed, namely: missions, admission headcounts, enrollment graduation rates and degrees conferred.

In the second half of this study, a transition is made to another source of data reporting and findings called "interviews." These interviews, composed of questions, comments and responses, will serve as the qualitative data obtained from the administrative leaders of Jackson State University. This researcher discusses the interview questions derived from the quantitative data as a means of providing information that gives an internal and personal understanding of desegregation as told through the eyes and hearts of those who serve the institution. A narrative format is used in which interview questions are presented and responses are recorded. These responses are then presented in a format that elaborates on inferences and implications relative to the initial research questions posed in Chapter One.

The Mississippi Institutions of Higher Learning focus on six strategic themes assessed by core indicators that they have determined to be paramount in preparing students to achieve their optimal educational goals. This council uses "System Core Indicators" to compare, assess and evaluate institutions statewide. "Institutional Core Indicators," on the other hand, are specifically used to assess an institution relative to the state's specific mandates for it. Both sets of indicators seek to measure Mississippi's postsecondary institutions (Table 4.1) in terms of educational quality in the areas of instruction, research and public service. In addition, the indicators are used in terms of measuring productivity, efficiency, equity and effectiveness.

Table 4.1

Mississippi Institutions of Higher Learning

Name	Abbreviation	Historical Population Type
Alcorn State University	(ASU)	HBCU
Delta State University	(DSU)	TWI
Jackson State University	(JSU)	HBCU
Mississippi State University	(MSU)	TWI
Mississippi University for Women	(MUW)	TWI
Mississippi Valley State University	(MVSU)	HBCU
University of Southern Mississippi	(USM)	TWI
University of Mississippi	(UM)	TWI

System Core Indicators

Faculty to Student Ratio

In terms of class size and academic quality, Jackson State University ranked third best (Table 4.2) with an average ratio of one full-time faculty member for every 17 students. The highest ratios in the state were held by DSU, UM, MVSU and UM. Although the state's TWIs were larger in faculty numbers and full-time equivalent students, JSU's low faculty-student ratio was a good indicator of quality learning being achieved. Statewide, class size averages 18. Faculty at JSU may be far more accessible and there is a greater chance of close immediate feedback, input and communication among faculty and students, which may give rise to higher quality academic learning.

Table 4.2

Ratio of Full-Time Faculty to Full Time Equivalent (FTE) Students

Institution	Faculty to FTE Students
ASU	1:15
DSU	1:18
JSU	1:17
MSU	1:15
MUW	1:13
MVSU	1:22
UM	1:20
USM	1:23
System	1:18

Source: Office of Research and Planning, Institute of Higher Learning, Mississippi (IHLMS)

Percent of Freshmen Enrolled

In terms of intermediate courses offered to help first-time freshmen who are under-prepared students with limited backgrounds, JSU reflected a 22.2% ranking it on the lower end at sixth place of the eight public institutions (Table 4.3). JSU (ranked fifth) is critically challenged in having students that are sufficiently prepared for college upon entrance. JSU has to do a better job of attracting better quality students, or it must provide extensive support to these students during their college experience to ensure graduation. Overall, 14% of all freshmen in Mississippi were enrolled in one or more intermediate classes.

Table 4.3

Percent of Freshmen Enrolled in Intermediate Classes

Institution	Freshmen Enrolled Fall 2001
ASU	23.5%
DSU	12.7%
JSU	22.2%
MSU	8.8%
MUW	12.2%
MVSU	19.3%
UM	9.0%
USM	18.3%
System	14.5%

Source: IHLMS.

Graduation Rates

In terms of overall graduation rates (first-time entering freshmen who graduate within six years) from 1990 to 1996, JSU and another HBCU, Mississippi Valley State University, both had the lowest graduation rates for full-time entering freshmen graduating within six years (Table 4.4). This finding suggests that JSU, like other HBCUs, lacks the necessary resources (monies, specialized support programs, etc.) that have negatively impacted the institution's ability to improve and ensure academic growth and success among its student population. Forty seven percent of first-time, full-time entering freshmen graduate within six years. It is clear that the lack of resources related to the desegregation lawsuit has impacted JSU.

Table 4.4
Six-Year Cohort Graduation Rate

Institution	Fall 1994	Fall 1995	Fall 1996
ASU	44.7%	42.3%	46.3%
DSU	41.0%	48.1%	42.3%
JSU	31.5%	31.4%	35.0%
MSU	47.2%	50.7%	52.1%
MUW	38.7%	38.5%	42.1%
MVSU	31.3%	37.7%	35.0%
UM	50.5%	50.4%	55.5%
USM	42.2%	44.4%	47.6%
System	43.0%	44.0%	47.6%

Source: Office of Research and Planning, Institutes of Higher Learning Management Information Systems (IHLMIS).

Affordability

The average tuition costs of college/university attendance in Mississippi are almost one-third of state per capita income. JSU is clearly economical in terms of dollars and cents spent for a student to attend. Jackson State University, at 33.1%, is the third highest in terms of costs and comparable to other institutions in the state as can be seen from Table 4.5.

Table 4.5
Average Tuition Cost to State per Capita Income

Institution	Tuition Cost In % of State Per Capita Income, FY 2002
ASU	27.8%
DSU	27.9%
JSU	33.1%
MSU	27.0%
MUW	28.1%
MVSU	
UM	34.1%
USM	32.1%
System	30.5%

Source: Offices of Finance and Administration

Accessibility

Student accessibility to the system's institutions of higher learning can be seen in terms of the overall headcount enrollment. In Fall 2001, JSU had an overall student headcount of 7,098, ranking it the fourth largest in terms of student population of the eight institutions as illustrated in Table 4.6. Clearly, a significant number of students attend JSU for several purposes and feel JSU has an essential mission in fulfilling their needs. The overall total FTE (full-time equivalent) enrollment statewide indicated that JSU further was consistent with maintaining a fourth-place overall ranking among the state's eight public institutions from 1999-2001.

Table 4.6
Total Enrollment

Institution	Fall 1999	Fall 2000	Fall 2001
ASU	2,871	2,936	3,096
DSU	4,086	3,916	3,875
JSU	6,356	6,832	7,098
MSU	16,076	16,561	16,878
MUW	2,953	2,815	2,328
MVSU	2,511	2.687	3,081
UM	11,746	12,234	12,771
USM	14,350	14,509	15,232
System	60,949	62,490	64,359

Source: Office of Research and Planning, IHLMIS.

Accountability/Funding

Jackson State University is primarily a teaching institution with a higher percentage of monies allocated for instruction. According to Table 4.7, JSU averaged sixth in terms of monies spent on instruction. This lack of funding and allocations from the state seriously impacts JSU's ability to provide greater service to its constituents.

Table 4.7
Institutional Budget Allocated for Instruction

Institution	FY1999	FY2000	FY2001
ASU	33.9%	32.7%	34.7%
DSU	38.7%	40.2%	38.6%
JSU	32.9%	28.0%	28.6%
MSU	21.6%	21.8%	17.0%
MUW	29.0%	30.7%	31.2%
MVSU	30.0%	28.5%	28.8%
UM	37.9%	38.1%	34.2%
USM	36.6%	36.6%	36.0%
System	30.4%	30.1%	27.8%

Source: Offices of Finance and Administration

In striving to make effective and efficient use of the state's resources for the primary purpose of providing students with a higher education, JSU ranked second statewide in terms of expenditures used for each full-time student (Tables 4.8 and 4.9). The data reveals that JSU essentially relies on state resources to ensure effectiveness in accommodating full-time students. Lack of funding from the state clearly is detrimental to JSU and its institutional effectiveness.

Table 4.8
Current Expenditures per FTE Student

Institution	$ per FTE Student
ASU	$18,101
DSU	$12,311
JSU	$19,622
MSU	$26,189
MUW	$15,807
MVSU	$14,283
UM	$18,787
USM	$18,971

Source: Office of Finance and Administration.

Table 4.9
Trend Data—Current Expenditures per FTE Student

Institution	FY 1999	FY 2000	FY 2001
JSU	$13,450	$18,204	$19,622
System	$16,192	$18,227	$18,971

Source: Office of Finance and Administration.

Mississippi spends an average of over $5,000 on instruction per FTE student. Jackson State University ranks fifth best in the state in terms of monies spent on the instruction of students (Table 4.10). These data also show that state-provided resources are heavily depended on by JSU. Without these fiscal resources, JSU would experience detrimental consequences in terms of cost-efficient instruction.

Table 4.10
Instructional Expenditures per FTE Student

Institution	$ per Student Spent on Instruction
ASU	$6,277
DSU	$5,752
JSU	$5,611
MSU	$4,440
MUW	$4,935
MVSU	$4,116
UM	$6,424
USM	$5,217
System	$5,270

Source: Offices of Finance and Administration, Instructional Program Educational Division Services (IPEDS).

The system considers instruction to be a cornerstone of higher education. Consequently, it strives to allocate a significant proportion of its fiscal resources toward the instruction of students. The system spends over $5,000, on average, for instruction per FTE student.

Degrees In Natural Sciences, Mathematics, Computer Science and Engineering

The number of degrees awarded in specific disciplines significantly impacts the state's economic development. JSU ranked fourth in the state for degrees granted in key specific disciplines in 2001. With a total of 220 degrees granted in the sciences, math, computers and engineering disciplines, these data indicate that JSU serves a vital mission in producing under-represented populations in key fields (Table 4.11). This is crucial because it lends support to the vital necessity of their continued existence as an institution with a specialized mission to serve historically disadvantaged citizens, see Table 4.12.

Table 4.11
Degrees in Natural Sciences, Mathematics, Computer Science and Engineering

Institution	Degrees Awarded FY 2001
ASU	129
DSU	55
JSU	220
MSU	966
MUW	28
MVSU	80
UM	304
USM	429

Table 4.12
Trend Data-Degrees In Natural Sciences, Mathematics, Computer Science and Engineering

	Number of Degrees Awarded		
Institution	FY 1999	FY 2000	FY 2001
JSU	259	203	220
System	2,164	2,146	2,211

Source: Office of Research and Planning, IHLMIS.

Degrees in Nursing and Health Sciences

JSU produced 34 degree recipients in 2001 in the fields of nursing and health sciences, seventh (Table 4.13). There is a vast need for JSU to be strengthened in these fields to compete on a statewide basis. This low degree production is an indication of JSU's restrictive mission by the state. Mississippi's medical university and TWIs draw most of the state's students to the health sciences and nursing fields.

Table 4.13
Degrees in Nursing and Health Sciences

	Number of Degrees Awarded		
Institution	FY 1999	FY 2000	FY 2001
ASU	47	49	44
DSU	73	46	62
JSU	11	30	34
MSU	62	67	63
MUW	100	106	122
MVSU	12	15	19
UM*	838	705	649
USM	366	380	355
System	1,509	1,398	1,348

* Includes the Medical Center
Source: Office of Research and Planning, IHLMIS.

Diversity

The number of degrees awarded to black and other minority students in Mississippi is reflected in Table 4.14. In 2002, the year the desegregation lawsuit was settled, JSU awarded 92.7% of its degrees to blacks, 4.6% to whites and 2.7% to other minorities. Such data reveal this institution produces a significant number of minority graduates. In contrast to the TWIs, the number of minorities receiving degrees averages less than 17% at the University of Mississippi, Southern Mississippi and the Mississippi University for Women. The data indicates clearly that Mississippi's TWIs lag far behind in producing minority degree recipients and that JSU serves as a crucial institution providing degrees to Mississippi's historically under-represented minority and disadvantaged population. System wide, JSU produced roughly one-third of all minority degrees in 2002.

Table 4.14
Degrees by Ethnicity

Degrees Awarded by Ethnicity

Institution	FY2000				FY2001				FY2002			
	White	Black	Other	Total	White	Black	Other	Total	White	Black	Other	Total
ASU	33	560	5	598	40	560	529	573	53	516	11	580
DSU	537	211	13	761	553	236	13	802	584	231	9	824
JSU	42	876	27	945	39	936	29	1,004	50	1,010	29	1,089
MSU	2,646	420	253	3,319	2,596	408	273	3,277	2,949	495	279	3,723
MUW	333	114	21	468	372	110	17	499	347	99	18	464
MVSU	6	345	1	352	8	318	1	327	11	394	4	409
UM	2,026	205	169	2,400	2,128	262	181	2,571	2,287	280	163	2,730
USM	2,701	552	151	3,404	2,797	550	150	3,497	2,754	594	150	3,498

Source: Office of Research and Planning, IHLMIS.

At this point, the researcher shifts from System wide core indicators to that of Institutional core indicators. These indicators reflect the educational quality offered within the institution relative to the state's mandate.

Institutional Core Indicators

Full-Time Faculty with Doctorate Degrees

JSU is within range of its total target goal set by the State of Mississippi in terms of acquiring an 80% rating by year 2007. From 1999 through 2001, JSU averaged a 73% rating (Table 4.15).

Table 4.15
Full-Time Faculty with Doctorate Degrees

Institution	Fall 1999	Fall 2000	Fall 2001	Target—by Year
MSU	68.6%	69.2%	72.2%	80%—2006
UM	80.4%	80.9%	80.8%	82%—2006
USM	73.1%	74.7%	75.6%	80%—2006
JSU	73.4%	73.7%	73.5%	80%—2007
ASU	56.7%	54.9%	59.3%	70%—2005
DSU	61.7%	60.6%	58.9%	75%—2005
MUW	60.6%	62.3%	58.2%	68%—2005
MVSU	54.5%	50.4%	55.9%	70%—2007

Source: Office of Research and Planning, IHLMIS.

Average ACT Score of First-Time Freshmen

In terms of average act scores of first-time freshmen, JSU reflects an average score of 18 (Table 4.16). The highest attainable score is 36. The national average is 21 and the state's average is 21. The lower ACT average at JSU may indicate why this institution has represented historically under-represented and disadvantaged minority citizens who stand in need of an institution who will seriously provide support and nurturing for college success.

Table 4.16
Average ACT Scores of First-Time Freshmen

| | Average   ACT Scores | | | |
Institution	Fall 1999	Fall 2000	Fall 2001	Target—by Year
MSU	23.3	23.1	23.5	24.1—2006
UM	23.3	23.3	22.9	24.1—2006
USM	21.6	21.5	20.9	22.0—2006
JSU	18.4	18.1	18.0	19.0—2007
ASU	18.2	17.6	17.5	19.0—2005
DSU	19.7	19.7	20.4	21.0—2003
MUW	21.7	21.5	21.8	21.8—2005
MVSU	17.5	17.2	16.7	19.0—2007

Source: Office of Research and Planning, IHLMIS.

Student Retention

According to the data in Table 4.17, JSU is averaging a consistent retention rate of 73.1% among its student population with a target goal set by the state at 75% for Fall 2007. Most other institutions in the state (both HBCUs and TWIs) range from 71% to 78.9%.

Table 4.17
Fall to Fall Cohort Retention Rate Year 2/Year 3

| | Fall 1997 | | Fall 1998 | | Fall 1999 | | System Target by Year | | |
| | Entering Freshme | | Entering Freshme | | Entering Freshmen | | | | |
Institution	Year 2	Year 3	Year 2	Year 3	Year 2	Year 3	Year 2	Year 3	By Date
MSU	76.6%	67.2%	78.6%	68.3%	78.9%	71.0%	80.0%	73.0%	2006
UM	75.1%	66.8%	75.0%	65.7%	75.9%	67.9%	80.0%	70.0%	2006
USM	71.4%	57.6%	71.4%	59.5%	69.3%	59.6%	80.0%	65.0%	2006
JSU	71.4%	58.4%	77.6%	66.4%	73.1%	61.6%	75.0%	65.0%	2007
ASU	71.1%	59.4%	70.3%	58.6%	73.6%	60.5%	75.0%	67.0%	2005
DSU	74.8%	65.0%	75.0%	56.3%	67.7%	58.3%	68.0%	58.0%	2002
MUW	74.0%	61.9%	64.3%	52.5%	67.0%	52.3%	73.5%	62.0%	2005
MVSU	70.8%	59.3%	75.3%	64.5%	73.8%	63.5%	76.0%	65.0%	2003

Source: Office of Research and Planning, IHLMIS.

Affordability

JSU's ranking of 12.8%-14.2% (Table 4.18) reflects a good overall under-graduate tuition fees standard for the citizens of Mississippi. The school is very affordable in terms of fees for a degree.

Table 4.18

Undergraduate Tuition and Required Fees to State Per Capita Income

Institution	Tuition & Fees to State Per Capita Income			
	FY 2000	FY 2001	FY 2002	Target—by Year
MSU	14.4%	14.3%	15.9%	15.0%—2006
UM	14.5%	14.5%	16.0%	15.0%—2006
USM	13.7%	13.7%	15.1%	16.0%—2006
JSU	12.8%	12.8%	14.2%	12.5%—2007
ASU	12.8%	12.8%	14.2%	15.0%—2005
DSU	12.4%	12.4%	13.7%	15.0%—2006
MUW	12.2%	12.2%	13.5%	15.0%—2006
MVSU	12.6%	12.6%	14.0%	13.0%—2007

Source: Office of Research and Planning, IHLMIS.

In terms of students receiving financial aid from the State of Mississippi, JSU has roughly 80% or more of students dependent on such funding (Table 4.19). Its viability as related to financing students for a college education is heavily tied to monies allocated by the State of Mississippi.

Table 4.19
Percentage of Students on Financial Aid

Institution	FY 1999	FY 2000	FY2001	Target	Year
MSU	77.8%	77.6%	78.9%	79%	2006
UM	72.6%	72.5%	71.6%	72%	2006
USM	71.4%	74.3%	75.6%	76%	2006
JSU	81.8%	83.1%	85.3%	85%	2007
ASU	84.0%	89.4%	84.7%	87%	2005
DSU	59.6%	65.4%	71.0%	80%	2008
MUW	79.7%	82.6%	89.7%	80-85%	2005
MVSU	92.3%	91.9%	95.3%	93%	2005

Source: Office of Research and Planning, IHLMIS.

Degrees in Natural Sciences, Mathematics, Computer Science, Engineering, Nursing and Health Sciences

Table 4.20 indicates that HBCUs produce a significant number of minorities in historically under-represented fields such as the natural sciences, mathematics, computer science, engineering, nursing and health related sciences. These institutions produce future professionals in under-represented areas.

Table 4.20

Degrees in Natural Sciences, Math, Computer Science, Engineering, Nursing, Health Science

Institution	Degrees Conferred				
	FY 1999	FY 2000	FY2001	Target by	Year
MSU				Bach-820	
	905	979	966		2006
NS/M/CS/Eng				Mast-50	
	62	67	63		
Nurs/Health				Prof-50	
				Doct-50	
UM				Bach-350	
	298	277	295		2006
NS/M/CS/Eng				Mast-80	
	234	227	202		
Nurs/Health				Prof-80	
				Doct-50	
USM				Bach-650	
	375	384	429		2006
NS/M/CS/Eng				Mast-175	
	366	380	355		
Nurs/Health				Doct-25	
JSU					
	259	203	220	Bach-365	2007
NS/M/CS/Eng					
	11	30	34	Mast-273	
Nurs/Health					
MUW					
	34	39	80	Bach-127	2006
NS/M/CS/Eng					
	100	106	19	Mast-38	
Nurs/Health					
MVSU					
	78	73	80	Bach-117	2007
NS/M/CS/Eng					
	12	15	19	Mast-35	
Nurs/Health					

Office of Research and Planning, IHLMIS.

Note: NS = Natural Sciences, M = Math, CS = Computer Science, Eng = Engineering, Nurs = Nursing.

Full-Time Faculty by Ethnicity

Data from Table 4.21 addresses the issue of the percent total of full-time faculty by ethnicity and gender. From the findings listed here, it is clear that HBCUs have the highest percentage of minorities (blacks and women) in terms of under-represented faculty statewide. The Mississippi minority state population is 33%. The state's TWIs do not reflect the 33% minority population of the state in terms of faculty. Further, the implication here is that HBCUs unquestionably serve a significant role in Mississippi providing minority faculty as role models and mentors for its minority population.

Table 4.21
Faculty by Ethnicity

Institution	Percent of Full-Time Faculty		
	Black	White	Other
MSU	1.9%-2.2%	29.1%-61.7%	1.2%-5.5%
UM	2.3%-3.1%	31.3%-60.9%	1.1%-4.9%
USM	1.1%-2.5%	97.0%-98.0%	0.1-2.0%
JSU	32.1%-34.3%	8.1%-11.0%	1.3%-11.1%
ASU	28.8%-34.2%	8.2%-14.4%	3.9%-11.4%
DSU	8.1%-23.3%	28.5%-38.8%	0.3%-0.7%
MUW	0.7%-3.7%	36.6%-57.7%	0.0%-3.0%
MVSU	27.7%-40.2%	2.7%-11.3%	0.9%-17.7%

Source: Office of Research and Planning, IHLMIS.

Students by Ethnicity

According to Mississippi's IHL, the total students by ethnicity and gender for minorities were found almost exclusively at the state's HBCUs (Table 4.22). The average TWI in Mississippi held an average composition of minority students between a low of 3.2% to a high of 24.4%. It is clear from this data that HBCUs hold most of the state's minority students pursuing a higher education.

Table 4.22
Students by Ethnicity

University	Percent of Students by Ethnicity, 2000-2002		
	Black	White	Other
MSU	6.4%-11.5%	32.8%-43.1%	2.5%-4.6%
UM	4.4%-8.3%	39.8%-42.3%	2.6%-3.2%
USM	6.1%-14.7%	31.3%-44.5%	2.1%-2.5%
JSU	34.3%-59.5%	1.1%-2.4%	0.0%-1.3%
ASU	35.5%-57.9%	0.9%-5.4%	0.4%-1.3%
DSU	8.1%-23.3%	28.5%-38.2%	0.4%-0.7%
MUW	2.8%-24.6%	11.3%-56.7%	0.6%-2.8%
MVSU	26.5%-63.2%	1.4%-2.9%	0.2%-0.7%

Source: Office of Research and Planning, IHLMIS.

Degrees by Ethnicity

In terms of degrees granted based on ethnicity (white/black/other), JSU was second in the State of Mississippi of eight public institutions in the years (2000-2002) in the total number of degrees awarded. Table 4.23 shows that Mississippi's HBCUs produced the highest number of degrees awarded to minorities. This finding confirms that these institutions are a source of significant production in terms of minorities or historically under-represented populations receiving a higher education in Mississippi. (MVSU: blacks 96%; JSU: blacks 93%; ASU: blacks 89%).

Although awarding the highest number of degrees by ethnicity among TWIs in Mississippi, the following institutions and their respective percentages reflect a serious shortcoming in their ability to produce minority graduates in significant numbers: Delta State University: blacks 28%; Mississippi University for Women: blacks 21%; University of Southern Mississippi: blacks 17%.

Table 4.23
Degrees by Ethnicity

| | Degrees by Ethnicity | | | | | | | | | | | |
| | FY 2000 | | | FY2001 | | | FY 2002 | | | System Target by Date | | |
Institution	W	B	O	W	B	O	W	B	O	W	B	O	Year
MSU	80%	13%	8%	79%	12%	8%	79%	13%	7%	78%	14%	8%	2006
UM	84%	9%	7%	83%	10%	7%	84%	10%	6%	82%	12%	6%	2006
USM	79%	16%	4%	80%	16%	4%	79%	17%	4%	79%	17%	4%	2006
JSU	4%	93%	3%	4%	93%	3%	5%	93%	3%	5%	93%	3%	2007
ASU	6%	94%	1%	7%	89%	1%	9%	89%	3%	11%	86%	3%	2007
DSU	71%	28%	2%	69%	29%	2%	71%	28%	1%	69%	29%	2%	2005
MUW	71%	24%	4%	75%	22%	3%	75%	21%	4%	73%	23%	4%	2006
MVSU	2%	98%	0%	2%	98%	0%	3%	96%	1%	5%	93%	2%	2005

Source: Office of Research and Planning, IHLMIS. Note: W = White, B = Black, O = Other

Missions

In evaluating the purpose and significance of an institution's mission, it is crucial to understand the institution's origin, the original state mandate and whether or not this has changed over the years. In addition, this study looked at each institution's mission in terms of goals and objectives and not exclusively in terms of a statistical comparison in which numbers were simply compared. If an institution is to exist solely to produce teachers, for example, it has to be looked at in the context for which it exists. The institution cannot be held accountable for other goals that it was not charged to reach. With this in mind, this researcher hoped to provide the reader with some sense of how the HBCUs originated and what they now exist to do, inclusive of any changes from their initial missions.

Alcorn State University

Alcorn State University (ASU), the oldest predominantly black land-grant university in the country, began in 1830 as Oakland College with the specific purpose of educating only white male students. The school was closed at the beginning of the Civil War and reopened later after being sold to African-Americans in response to the Congressional ruling which gave rise to the Morrill Land-Grant Act of 1862. Its name changed to Alcorn Agricultural and Mechanical College in 1878, and it was later renamed Alcorn State University (1974). Since its second-inception mandate by the State of Mississippi was to serve African-Americans, it continues to exist as a co-educational, land-grant, liberal arts, science and teacher education public institution. Its sole purpose to this day has been to continue providing instructional programs resulting in associate, baccalaureate, master and educational specialist degree completions. This institution which started out serving only white male constituents—is now predominantly black (89.0%), with 9.1% white students and 1.9% other race students—and opens it doors to all races and both genders. It is obvious that this institution's mission changed from its original charter and to embraces a mission focused primarily on educating traditionally disadvantaged populations (African-Americans), and yet it continues to recruit and educate non-blacks.

Delta State University

Delta State University (DSU) was founded originally in 1924 as a teacher's college to build a supply of instructors for the State of Mississippi. This institution has revised its mission to include a comprehensive undergraduate curriculum focused on serving the "Delta Region" of Mississippi which is composed of rural, ethnically diverse and non-urban residents.

Jackson State University

Founded in 1877 by Baptist missionaries, Jackson State University was initially a private church school with only 20 students, whose sole purpose was to serve the Mississippi Valley between Memphis, Tennessee, and the Gulf Coast. JSU relocated to Jackson in 1882 and trained only teachers. After 1953 this institution expanded its mission by embracing graduate programs and advancing a more comprehensive undergraduate curriculum. In 1979, JSU was designated by the State of Mississippi as an urban university to fulfill its new mission of offering public service programs to address the problems of urban life and city environments. Over the years, it has become the state's flagship black institution, offering 43 bachelor degree programs, 38 master degree programs, 6 specialist degree programs and 9 doctoral degree programs, for a total of 96 degree programs.

Compared to TWIs in the State, JSU, ranks fourth in number of degrees and instructional programs offered. It follows USM with 187, MSU with 181 and Ole Miss with 146. Such data makes JSU a pivotal state institution. Its mission has changed from providing agricultural, mechanical and industrial-vocational training to that of providing a strong comprehensive curriculum mandated to address urban issues and challenges and the needs of African-Americans who pursue higher education in the liberal arts, business and the sciences (engineering, biology and chemistry, etc.).

Mississippi State University

MSU began as the Agricultural and Mechanical College of the State of Mississippi, one of the national land-grant colleges established through the Morrill Act of 1862. It was created by Mississippi's legislature on February 28, 1878, to fulfill the mission of offering training in "agriculture, horticulture and the mechanical arts without excluding other scientific and classical studies, including military tactics."

Through the Hatch Act (1887) and the Smith Lever Act (1914), this institution took on the mission of providing agricultural and home economics programs to nonresidents through distance learning offered through extension offices. Renamed Mississippi State University in 1958, it has today refined its mission and serves to offer high quality research and liberal education at the bachelor, master, professional and doctoral levels.

Mississippi University for Women

Established in 1884, this institution became the first public college for women in America. Originally known as the Industrial Institute and College, it sought to provide a liberal arts education and prepare women for employment. It changed its name in 1920, emphasizing collegiate rather than vocational education. MUW expanded its mission to become an institution of quality academic programs open to both females and males with emphasis on "distinctive opportunities for women." This institution continues to function in a specialized role to meet the needs of women, without excluding men.

Mississippi Valley State University

MVSU was created by Mississippi's legislature as Mississippi Vocational College in 1946. Its initial purpose and mission were to train African-American teachers for rural and elementary schools and to provide vocational training. In 1964, its name was changed to embrace its mission change to general and special higher education opportunities for African-Americans in diverse academic programs. Today, it maintains its original role while also providing expanded undergraduate and graduate programs.

University of Mississippi Medical Center

Established in 1903 in Oxford, Mississippi, UMMC was initially a medical school offering only basic science courses for two years. Students then transferred out of state for two additional years of clinical training. The school was ultimately moved to Jackson and became an established 4-year medical school fully equipped with research, library and teaching hospital status. Its mission further expanded as a health center embracing the health-related professions, a school of dentistry and a hospital for the citizens of Mississippi.

University of Mississippi

"Ole Miss," or UM, was founded in 1844 with the mission of providing a strong liberal arts education for the white citizens of Mississippi. In subsequent years, it broadened its mission by creating professional and specialized schools. Its mission afterwards was refined to fulfill the status of the Mississippi flagship institution, providing the most comprehensive education in the state. Offering over 100 academic programs that lead to careers in engineering, business, telecommunications, politics, journalism, pharmacy, law, medicine, dentistry, accounting, education and health-related professions, etc., its mission is clearly defined.

University of Southern Mississippi

This university was founded in 1910 and evolved as another major comprehensive university to serve the needs of southern Mississippians. Its mission has been redefined over the years to provide extensive academic programming and residential experience for its students. USM evolved to earn a national reputation as a "research institution" and university for primarily graduate education.

Missions Summary Analysis and Related Core Indicators

In essence, these institutions all originated with specific, distinct missions. Based on changing demographics including political, social and economic factors, the institutions' missions now range from "general" to "comprehensive." Those with general missions offer general academic programs, while those with missions denoting special needs or opportunities provide education, training and services for specific populations based on gender and race. With flexible admissions policies and practices, these institutions are able to exist without excluding others on the basis of gender and race. In addition, their educationally justified continued existence is strongly predicated on their mission, purpose and goals. These institutions serve clearly stated missions that indicate "medical" or "comprehensive" as well as "research-graduate." Consequently, it is clear that they have existed and continue to exist on the basis of sound educational purposes regardless of their racial pasts. It is therefore logical and practical to conclude as well that HBCUs should also continue to exist as "special purpose" or "specialized institutions" serving specific populations without excluding race and gender.

As reflected in the mission statements, the Mississippi Institutions of Higher Learning has clear, distinct purposes for its institutions, and many of those missions have changed over the years since the respective institution's inception. Also noted is that the Council focuses on specific strategic themes or core indicators that are paramount in accomplishing the task of preparing students to achieve their optimal educational goals.

Further analysis of the quantitative data suggest that there is more compelling evidence for the continued existence of HBCUs, particularly Jackson State University. The specific areas outlined in this study (admissions enrollment, graduation rates and degrees, degrees conferred and instructional programs) suggest that there is evidence of challenges as well as successes to support this premise.

Student Enrollment

Student enrollment in undergraduate programs at the eight universities (not including University of Mississippi Medical Center) increased by 8.4% or 4,022 from 1995 to 2000. During this five-year period, undergraduate enrollment increased at five of the eight universities (Table 4.24). On the graduate level, total student enrollment at the eight universities increased by 1,119 or

10%. JSU saw an 8.2% increase overall in student enrollment primarily concentrated at the graduate level but without significant loss or decrease in student attendance on the undergraduate level. This finding suggests that JSU is able to maintain its goal of educating a primarily African-American population despite economic hardships. Four, or half, of the institutions lost enrollment. Three TWIs (DSU, which has a 25% African-American population, MUW and UMC) each lost a significant number of students. The three other predominantly white institutions saw gains (MSU +15.3%, Ole Miss +15.1%, and USM +6.2%). The state's two major HBCUs gaining significant enrollment were JSU at 8.2% and MVSU at 24.7%. Only one HBCU, Alcorn State, lost enrollment (-3.2%).

Table 4.24
Student Enrollment, Fall 1995-2000

Institution	1995			2000			% Change Over 5 Years
	Undergraduate	Graduate	Total	Undergraduate	Graduate	Total	
ASU	2,763	270	3,033	2,398	538	2,936	-3.12%
DSU	3,341	666	4,007	3,384	532	3,916	-2.3%
JSU	5,491	822	6,313	5,479	1,353	6,832	+8.2%
MSU	11,567	2,801	14,368	13,307	3,254	16,561	+15.3%
MUW	2,860	201	3,061	2,662	153	2,815	-8.0%
MVSU	2,139	15	2,154	2,358	329	2,687	+24.7%
UM	8,149	2,484	10,633	8,149	2,484	10,633	+15.1%
USM	10,939	2,718	13,657	12,143	2,366	14,509	+6.2%
Total	47,884	11,159	59,043	51,906	12,278	64,184	8.7%

Source: Office of Research and Planning, Institutions of Higher Learning Management Information System (IHLMIS).

Student Enrollment by Race, Gender and Residence

In looking at the overall data findings obtained for this study, Mississippi's public institution enrollment by race indicated significant progress for HBCUs (Table 4.25). The statistics were consistent with headcount enrollment by level for both black and white institutions. White enrollment increased by 4.7%, black enrollment by 16.0% and enrollment of other-race students increased by 15.1% over the five-year period from 1995-2000.

More whites also attended JSU than in the past, reflecting a 13.6% growth. JSU attracted and sustained more white students than in the past, creating a more diverse, multicultural student population to serve.

1. The total number of students enrolled in the eight universities increased by 5,141

2. students or 8.7% from Fall 1995 to the Fall 2000.

3. Overall, white enrollment increased 4.7%, black enrollment increased 16% and

4. enrollment by other-race students increased 15.1% over the five-years.

5. Black enrollment at the TWIs increased by a total of 9,632 students, an increase

6. of 28.3% Fall 1995 to Fall 2000.

Table 4.25
Student Enrollment by Race

University	1995				2000			
	White	Black	Other	Total	White	Black	Other	Total
ASU	180	2,836	17	3,033	207	2,691	38	2,936
DSU	2,922	1031	54	4,007	2,687	1,189	40	3,916
JSU	169	5,932	212	6,313	192	6,475	165	6,832
MSU	11,187	2,179	1,002	14,368	12,371	30,061	1,184	16,561
MUW	2,294	705	62	3,061	1,980	751	84	2,815
MVSU	18	2,132	4	2,154	112	2,554	21	2,687
UM	8,812	1,085	736	10,633	10,034	1,487	713	12,234
USM	10,820	2,361	476	13,657	10,791	3,029	689	14,509
Total	37,928	18,408	2,707	59,043	39,717	21,352	3,115	64,184

Source: Office of Research and Planning, IHLMIS.

Of the 64,184 students in the system as of 2000, 79.4% were residents of Mississippi: representing 18,764 or 36.8% black students, 31,003 or 60.9% white students and 1,162 or 2.3% other-race students (Table 4.26). Of these Mississippi residents, 30,374 or 59.6% were female and 20,555 or 40.4% were male. JSU reflected a 19.9% positive change in enrollment from residents of Mississippi. Compared to the state's TWIs, JSU ranked third of eight in terms of attracting state residents attending postsecondary institutions in Mississippi. This good news suggests that JSU is quite capable of attracting a significant segment of the state's mostly black population and an increasing percentage of whites who obviously have insignificant or few issues in attending an HBCU. Further observed from the data was the finding that JSU held the highest percent change (+266.7%) in terms of undergraduate headcount enrollment with students age 25 and over (non-traditional students) at off-campus locations. When compared to TWIs in Mississippi, JSU was ranked first in this category followed by Ole Miss with the second highest percentage (+232.0%). No other institutions (black or white) reflected such large triple-digit increases.

1. Of 64,184 students in the system, 79.4% are Mississippi residents.

2. Of total students in the system, 36.8% are black, 60.9% are white, and 2.3% are of other races.

3. By gender, 59.6% are female and 40.4% are male.

Table 4.26
System-Wide Headcount by Race-Fall 2000

	White	Black	Other
Headcount by Race	31,003	18,764	1,162
Headcount by % of Race	60.9%	36.8%	2.3%

Table 4.27 reflects total headcount enrollment by residence as follows:

1. Total resident student enrollment increased by 4,463 students or 9.6% from Fall Session 1995 to Fall Session 2000.

2. During the five-years, resident enrollment increased at five of the eight universities.

3. Total nonresident student enrollment increased by 678 students or 5.4% from Fall 1995 to Fall 2000.

Table 4.27
Student Enrollment by Residence

	Resident			Non-Resident		
Institution	1995	2000	% Change	1995	2000	% Change
ASU	2,651	2,523	-4.8%	382	413	+8.1%
DSU	2,752	3,614	-3.7%	255	302	+18.4%
JSU	4,528	5431	+19.9%	1,785	1,401	-21.5%
MSU	11,332	12,581	+11.0%	3,036	3,980	+31.1%
MUW	2,834	2,514	-11.3%	227	301	+32.6%
MVSU	1,913	2,512	+31.3%	241	175	-27.4%
UM	6,682	8,081	+20.9%	3,951	4,153	+5.1%
USM	11,235	12,287	+9.4%	2,422	2,222	-8.3%
Total	46,466	50,929	+9.6%	12,577	13,255	+5.4%

Source: Office of Research and Planning, IHLMIS.

Degrees Conferred by Race

Over the 6-year period from 1994 to 2002, the overall system saw an increase of 8.8% degrees conferred. The number of degrees earned by black students increased by 772 or 30.2%. A closer analysis of the data indicates that this significant growth occurred primarily at the state's HBCUs. Jackson State University saw a jump of 61.5% in degrees conferred to whites. On one hand, this is good news because it shows significant progress not only in attacting white students but also in that they stayed to graduate. On the other hand, during this same time period, JSU only saw a 4.3% increase in degrees conferred to its black students. This result is a mixture of good and bad. More blacks did graduate from JSU, however, the much smaller and less-comprehensive HBCUs (ASU with a 37.3% increase in degrees conferred to its black students and MVSU with a 55.4% increase) actually produced more graduates in both numbers and percentage of headcount. Further, these same institutions actually lost numbers and percentages among their white students having degrees conferred. Further signs of problems can found by an analysis of the data reflected by Tables 4.28 and 4.29.

Table 4.28
Total Degrees Conferred to White Students

University	1994-1995	1999-2000	% Change
ASU	55	33	-40.0%
DSU	612	537	-12.3%
JSU	26	42	+61.5%
MSU	2,374	2,646	+11.5%
MUW	375	333	-11.2%
MVSU	0	6	N/A
UM	1,885	2,026	+7.5%
USM	2,615	2,701	+3.3%
Total	8,405	8,754	+4.2%

Source: IHLMIS.

Table 4.29
Degrees Conferred by Race

	1994-1995			1999-2000		
University	Black	White	Other	Black	White	Other
ASU	408	55	8	560	33	5
DSU	169	612	9	211	537	13
JSU	840	26	31	876	42	27
MSU	294	2,374	311	420	2,646	253
MUW	78	375	3	114	333	21
MVSU	22	0	1	345	6	1
UM	169	1,885	217	205	2,026	169
USM	326	2,615	153	552	2,701	151
Total	2,553	8,405	748	3325	8,754	660

Source: Institutions of Higher Learning Management Information System.

Graduation Rates of Entering Freshmen

As reflected in Table 4.30, five of the eight universities had an average graduation rate above 40%. The Mississippi system average was 45.9% during the desegregation period 1985-1994. Jackson State University only produced an average of 32. 4%, ranking it seventh among eight state universities. This finding confirms the serious retention problem that JSU has had to continuously address. Although the number of students attending JSU increased over these years, the institution still struggles to resolve its student retention problem.

Table 4.30
Graduation Rates of Entering Freshmen

University	1985	1986	1987	1988	1989	1990	1991	1992	1993	1994	Avg.
ASU	32.4	34.8	32.0	37.1	37.5	35.3	38.8	43.7	52.2	49.3	39.3
DSU	50.8	54.6	52.7	52.5	51.5	52.4	50.6	46.3	47.8	51.3	51.1
JSU	29.0	36.2	34.6	33.9	33.5	32.6	30.0	30.4	30.6	32.8	32.4
MSU	55.1	56.0	56.3	55.2	56.0	51.1	53.5	54.1	54.3	51.8	54.3
MUW	45.6	51.7	53.5	50.2	49.6	39.8	49.8	43.5	43.3	47.5	47.5
MVUS	25.7	28.3	33.1	33.4	27.6	24.9	23.9	30.0	30.3	33.4	29.1
UM	51.6	54.7	56.3	53.8	53.7	52.2	52.3	49.5	53.4	54.6	53.2
USM	43.0	42.5	47.4	46.9	47.0	46.9	40.4	39.6	43.1	46.3	44.3
System	44.5	47.3	47.9	47.3	46.8	44.4	44.0	44.2	45.9	47.1	45.9

Source: IHLMIS

Note that each entering freshman cohort was tracked for six years to determine the rate of graduation for those students receiving degrees from any institution in the IHL in Mississippi. (Six years is considered a standard period of time for graduation according to the U.S Department of Education.)

The Interviews and Analyses

It is at this juncture that the final data in this study address perceptions of the gatekeepers at Jackson State University—the front-line administrators and staff members handling day-to-day administrative issues who experienced the impact of desegregation firsthand during the course of 26 years. The final desegregation rulings came in Spring 2002, leaving divided opinions about the welfare of Jackson State University in the aftermath. Both support and opposition remain just as strong after the final desegregation legal battle as before and during the process. In a moment, the reader will see clearly that the interview responses attest to this analysis. (See Appendix: Interview Questions.)

It is also important to understand that in evaluating the strengths of the two positions on the survival of HBCUs, particularly Jackson State University, it is necessary to examine what evidence exists to justify the continuance or discontinuance of this institution from the internal perceptions held by the institution's leadership. These internal views give rise to major themes, issues, interview questions and trends that are observed from analyzing the state's statistical data and institutional perceptions which form the focus of this chapter. Three distinct themes or perceptions derived from the interview data will be discussed. Theme identification, one of the most fundamental tasks in qualitative research, will also be discussed; it is one of the most mysterious and ambiguous, as well (Ryan, 1999). By themes, this researcher means abstract, often fuzzy and emotional perceptions or constructs which investigators often identify before, during and after data collection. Such themes or social perceptions emerge from various sources inclusive of literature reviews, the characteristics of the phenomena being studied, already agreed-upon professional definitions, local common-sense constructs and from actual people in the study (Maxwell, 1996). Another crucial element giving rise to themes originates from the researcher's own values, theoretical orientation and personal experiences with the subject matter (Mishler, 1991).

Explicit descriptions of theme discovery are rarely described in articles and reports. If so, they are often regulated to the categorization of appendices and footnotes (Bochner, 1994). This chapter examines how the data findings from the Mississippi Council on Higher Learning Annual Reports, the SACS Accreditation 10 Year Report of 2002 and the institution's own self-study are viewed from within the institution, not only from a statistical viewpoint, but also from social perceptions as experienced and expressed by the gatekeepers who are charged with implementing policies, court rulings and administrative decisions to ensure institutional effectiveness. An institution's internal self-image is pivotal to its ability to provide quality learning and fulfill its mission; internal conflicts can prevent growth and long solvency.

If all players are not in agreement with or in support of the vision, the institution runs the risk of self-destruction. How an institution feels about its president's vision, its historical contributions, its state legislature, its state oversight council and its social role to its immediate community, affects its functions in terms of leadership, instruction, faculty morale, community respect and student outcomes (Tinto, 1990). Not every theme, issue and trend will be discussed, but several major issues of institutional effectiveness as related to the mission of Jackson State University will be addressed. Not all interview question responses will be literally recorded, but certainly the major interview questions relevant to the issue of institutional effectiveness will be addressed.

For Jackson State University to have a continuing role and responsibility in meeting the needs of African-Americans in Mississippi as well as its other, non-black, citizens, it will need to address the views, values and convictions of those who lead the institution to fulfill its state-mandated mission

In interpreting the data, three major themes were discovered from the interviews conducted and observed as a result of the methodology used. Such themes or internal perceptions need detailed discussion for thorough understanding regarding the impact of desegregation. These themes or social perceptions are important in understanding what the present and possible future role of Jackson State University will be, in practical terms, towards fulfilling its mission. The camps or parties involved were asked several basic interview questions which allowed for an emergence of additional related issues, sub-theme questions and concerns not clearly seen in quantitative data.

This researcher assumes that the reader is well informed that black people are not monolithic in their thinking. Their views are as varied and extreme as any other population or ethnic group in the country. Some are integrationists at heart but lack the access and support to fully embrace such a position. Others are anti-integrationist and do not intend on integrating with anyone for any reason. There are others, of course, who are neither pro-integrationist nor anti-integrationist and represent a silent or seldom-heard voice among people of color. They take no prisoners, neither do they wish to be imprisoned. They simply want to survive without any major conflicts, confrontations and compromises.

The ideology or philosophical viewpoints of African-Americans who embrace integrationism often see such a position as both a means of survival and sustainability in an oppressive society. History has shown the inevitable evolution of minorities in many cultures who accept, support and cooperate in efforts to foster and perpetuate the dominant or majority culture's vision and values (Franklin, 1990). Subsequently, it is not uncommon to find African-Americans who see the fight for survival in America as one that must include assimilation into the mainstream through education, socialization, culture and the political process. This, of course, means mutual and cooperative assistance, presence and support from whites. On the other hand, there are those who stand in direct opposition to assimilation. These proponents see the necessity to maintain one's own history, values, beliefs and social customs by any means necessary; to integrate is to commit social suicide. History has taught them that any compromise and any cooperative effort results in detriment, destruction and death of the minority. They are called anti-integrationists.

Equally important is the existence of so called "neutralists" who are often seen as compromisers because they neither vocally nor visibly support one position over another. Their position assumes one of the viewpoints or philosophies will eventually dominate, and they will embrace it eventually, although perhaps reluctantly. During the process of conducting interviews to ascertain the social perceptions of Jackson State University administrators and staff, three major social perceptions, themes or camps emerged. Each group or camp revealed and reflected views that shed light on supportive and conflicting stands as to the impact of desegregation and the future role of Jackson State University.

Theme One: Towards a Non-Racially Identifiable Existence

The Supreme Court ruled that Jackson State University's desegregation legal battle in Mississippi was over on April 23, 2002. After 26 years of legal, political and social battles, the terms of the Court decree explicitly stated the allocation of $500 million overall to three of Mississippi's HBCUs with Jackson State University receiving $300 million over the next 17 years. The remaining $200 million would be divided equally between the two remaining smaller and less comprehensive HBCUs, Mississippi Valley State University and Alcorn State University. The vast majority of the financial resources were made available to enhance Jackson State University in several key areas: facilities, technological programs and services, student recruitment and retention, and curriculum development.

Over the years, Jackson State University has seen its roles and responsibilities change through several administrations. Originally conceived to meet only the primary needs of African-Americans as a transitional high school, it was later transformed by the Mississippi State Legislature into an industrial-technical institution to address the needs of a rural Mississippi black society in the early 1900s. Ironically, it once served as the academic haven of higher learning for minority students in Mississippi for most of the twentieth century. It is now mandated to attract an increasing number of white students as "minorities" with specialized assistance via scholarships, programs and set-asides to ensure racial diversity for its new post-desegregation role. Consequently, a battle has emerged over the extent of its black-white composition in terms of administration, faculty and student populations. The issue of being more or less black or diverse has been the paralyzing issue that remains unresolved. Leaders of Jackson State University and state higher education officials generally agree that increasing diversity is an important goal at both HBCUs and TWIs in Mississippi.

The 1992 decision known as *U.S. v. Fordice* directed states to eliminate policies and practices that keep public colleges racially identifiable. In essence, HBCUs were required to be less black and TWIs were required to be more racially inclusive and multicultural via student populations, programs, faculty and administrators, staff, services and activities. But the institutions and state officials have often disagreed on how much emphasis should be placed on that objective. Against the backdrop of numerical diversity goals and the physical enhancement of campus buildings and facilities tied to state aid, not all is well at Jackson State University. Since the recent Court decision ending the legal desegregation of Jackson State University its current president is supported by administrators, faculty and staff who support his vision to achiever higher standards.

These "integrationists" are composed of several administrators and some faculty members as well as staff specialists primarily educated at TWIs but who have served at HBCUs. They see the value and sociological benefit of HBCUs but they also embrace the majority white culture's goals and objectives for Jackson State University to be identical to Mississippi's TWIs. Their support of JSU in light of the impact of desegregation is to accept the $300 million financial package over the next 17 years to enhance Jackson State University. Although they feel shortchanged in terms of monies allocated by the Court ruling, their views and values are to push JSU towards the highest level of academic standards regardless of race and color.

How would you describe the impact of desegregation on Jackson State University in terms of overall institutional effectiveness and learning?

This question was asked by the researcher for respondents to describe the impact of desegregation in their own terms and from their own viewpoints. The interviewees were asked about learning, academic standards, instructional programs and having the means to achieve their institutional goals and missions. For example, one vice-provost stated: "I was educated at a white institution and, having worked at both HBCUs and TWIs for over 25 years, I am at a point were I just want to have quality learning, high academics and any resources we can get."

When asked whether Jackson State University was serving its purpose and fulfilling its mission, another vice-provost also conveyed that the desegregation impact "hit us hard." "Everybody was affected in some kind of way. We had to re-evaluate who we were and what we wanted to become. The eyes of the nation were upon us, and we knew the whole world was looking at us. Sometimes it got so confusing, we were trying to do the mission and safeguard our image with little resources. Hey, it's been an uphill battle all the way, but we still made strides."

Another top-level administrator responded to the question regarding the impact of desegregation when she stated, "I can remember when JSU was a horror to look at. Security was pathetic and the buildings were in disgrace. You know, it was kind of hard to work with an attitude of excellence when morale was low, the buildings were not up to par and then we didn't have computer technology. They paid us nothing and we didn't have any good way to be effective in educating students. Now, we have the right goals and objectives but then we didn't have money and the programs to do what we needed to do. If you ask me, we (Jackson State University) have made it against the odds and in spite of these insufficiencies. We just want to excel like everybody else. I mean, all the white institutions in Mississippi are doing it."

Ultimately, they seek to compete and to compare with Mississippi's TWIs as simply just another institution better able to serve its citizens. While these integrationists are on board, Jackson State University, under the current administration, will not disregard its historical role for black education in Mississippi. It will neither deny its historically black heritage nor totally seek to be completely integrated. Their position is obvious. They feel that due to the natural and historical order of socialization in America, Jackson State University, like other HBCUs, will continue to have a significant black population constituency. These leaders feel it is an issue that does not require direct action. For the integrationists, even with affirmative action efforts that result in increasing white student populations classified as minorities with scholarships, the institution will still continue to serve its historical role. According to them, it's a given. Nothing in that context needs to change. Jackson State University, accordingly, must simply aim to achieve higher standards comparable to Mississippi's TWIs. For these leaders, Jackson State University has served its historical purpose, but it needs a new image, a new role and a re-defined mission.

Three mid-level administrators voiced their sentiment as: "I don't give a damn about what the whites think. People used to look at us as a dangerous campus with students that don't do anything except party and play. We've gotten away from that kind of image, and I don't want us to go back to it."

What are your perceptions of Jackson State University in terms of image and mission before, during and after the desegregation experience...and the public's perceptions?

One mid-level administrator voiced, "I used to hate to come to this place because whenever you heard the name of JSU it was always associated with some crime and something negative. The media is always looking for the negative about us. We got crime, Ole Miss got crime, but you know who they are going to put on the front page."

Another mid-level administrator who works in admissions responded with the following: "Personally, I'm glad we have gone after better quality students, because we used to get non-college-prepared children who didn't want to learn, study or succeed. It's just good now to see good students black or white." She further stated, "We don't worry about the image of us being black. We can't change it. But you know that there are good black schools and bad black schools. There are good white students and bad white students. We got good black students and bad black students. So what? As long as we produce students that cut the mustard and graduate, we are happy. Our record of success speaks for us. We succeed in black and white either way you cut it."

This researcher noted during the interview that the integrationists stop short of viewing and wanting Jackson State University to be a completely non-racially identifiable institution. But they believe its future is secure with a mission that defines itself as one that has long served its historical role but now needs to move toward uncharted waters. Their mission is to raise the academic standards; attract quality students; access and acquire technology, programs and services that portray Jackson State University as an institution of higher learning with similar goals and objectives as Mississippi's TWIs.

They believe it is possible to maintain its rich history of black culture and yet acquire a new image and public perception that Jackson State University is user friendly and acceptable to the white citizens of Mississippi. Their motto is, "give us the chance and the choice," and we have a future for all regardless of color, race and ethnicity. Through strategic measures such as (a) strengthening the core curricula through programs of systematic assessment, (b) expanding technology to the African-American community and Mississippi by an inventory of courses taught via interactive video and distance learning, (c) embracing white students and other non-African-American students as valuable human resources for its own survival, (d) continuously upgrading and maintaining the quality of academic programs to comply with both internal and external approval and accreditation standards, (e) implementing and expanding specific programs and support systems to address to student retention and student success, and (f) giving the institution a physical face-lift, they argue JSU has a present and a future.

With these considerations in mind, the integrationists' strategy is to court the Council on Higher Education of Learning in Mississippi and the Mississippi State Legislature on the premise that Jackson State University is here to stay and has a viable role to play to all persons, regardless of color.

According to the integrationists, Jackson State University is composed of 95% African-American student population. There is a need to be more inclusive of non-black and foreign students as seen in their predominantly white graduate schools and non-traditional programs such as nursing and computers, etc. Their survival is predicated on the need to live in two worlds merged into one, which neither compromises nor totally submits (commonly viewed as "a sellout" or a person who disowns one's culture and history in exchange for another). Many of the integrationists on campus recall the negative and hostile images of Jackson State over the years. Inadequate facilities, insufficient state aide, deficient community support and political repercussions of fighting a legislature that neither respected them nor fully desired to acknowledge their presence or successes.

Entangled within this complex position is the reality that the integrationists place the blame equally on two sides, the state and the institution. Their rationale is simple: Much is to be blamed on Jackson State University because of partially self-inflicted actions such as crime, poor academics, less-qualified faculty and poor-quality students attending and dropping out, leaving a deficient graduation history. Equally to blame are the obvious, deliberate negligence and evasion by the State of Mississippi to fully fund, support and appreciate its historical role via funding equities and other resources. Consequently, the vision of the integrationists is to improve and to sustain Jackson State University as a quality institution for the twenty-first century.

Why do a lot of students enter JSU but not graduate, and how is JSU addressing the poor student retention rate?

To get a more concrete understanding and a clearer view of what Jackson State University has struggled with regarding institutional effectiveness, this researcher asked its director of institutional research to comment about Jackson State University's poor retention rate and the fact that the data reported by the Institution of Higher Learning (IHL) indicates a comparatively poor attrition rate, degree completion rate and achievement at JSU. Many students are admitted and attend but very few graduate. The respondent stated, "JSU has identified student retention as a serious issue and problem. We know that many of our kids come to college ill-prepared and academically deficient. But we also know that there are other variables like poor family support, inadequate financial assistance from their families and poor study habits, skills and efforts that cause them to fail. Some of them lack the mentoring and the tutorial assistance needed. Some of them are first generation college attendees, and you know what that means. Then there are some that had poor preparation at the high school level. They come to us not being able to read and write and comprehend beyond the tenth grade level. Some do not graduate because they have to work to support themselves while going to school; that's a problem. How do you tell students not to work when they need the money? They are just trying to juggle two or three hats at one time with little or no support. Some students have no parental involvement and therefore come to college not knowing what it is they really want to do. We have counselors and advisors, but if you haven't thought a lot of about the future, it's still hard to stick to that one major. Some students don't belong here. They are not college material and it's an issue nobody wants to talk about. They came here to get away from home but didn't have a plan to stay or succeed. They were just going to 'wing it.' But then I think I need to mention to you that some don't graduate because they have issues that require professional therapy and counseling. And you know, we are not in that kind of business. I guess what I am trying to say is that a lot of their problems cannot be changed overnight. It takes time and four years is sometimes just not enough time. But through programs to foster higher test scores and admissions standards, enrichment support programs, faculty mentoring initiatives, student-tailored retention strategies, programs and policies, and student based assessment strategies, we do see a difference. Sometimes these students drop in and they drop out and they come back, because they have other issues they are dealing with. But one thing about the data you cannot deny and that is the numbers may not be high but they are significant because these students started out low but look at how many did finish. I know it took five and six and seven years for some of them to do, it but they did finish. If you ask me, we are doing what we are supposed to do. We can do it better if we have the resources."

This researcher acknowledged, based upon the remarks and tones expressed by the director of institutional research, that it was a "sensitive subject" and certainly not meant to insult the institution. The director wanted to make sure it was understood that the statistics don't tell the whole story. This researcher further acknowledged that HBCUs in general have this problem, and it was obvious that they (at JSU) were trying to do something about it and that the intent was to help, not to embarrass the institution.

Another key mid-level administrator was asked to comment about the typical profile of a student at JSU and how JSU students differ from those attending TWIs in Mississippi. What was their feeling on whether or not the Council on Higher Learning data told the real desegregation impact story about JSU? The administrator commented, "Our typical student is someone who is black, female, poor, graduated in the low 10% to 40% of the class and doesn't have too much of a clue about what she came to college to study and succeed in. Our students are usually first generation and certainly no more than second generation. They lack the mentoring and the family connections, resources and ability to talk with someone about college. If we don't get them financial aid, they will not make it anywhere else. When they don't make it, then everybody blames them or us. I know we have counselors and advisors, but you have to understand that when you are the first to come to college there are so many pressures and distractions to achieve and succeed. These students need a personal interest taken in them, and they need to know they can make it regardless. We really don't care what color they are. We just want to get them up to high standards to make it. We want this college to have the reputation and the image that when you come out of here…you know something, you're good stock and the best quality money can buy. I just don't understand why that is so hard to understand and to have. All we ever asked the state to do was to give us what we were due. We have seen it happen year after year. Hell, I'm one of them who made it, and I was in the same boat as one of them. And if you want to really know the difference between our students and the ones that go everywhere else, it's simple. The students that go to Ole Miss and the others are rich, well-prepared, probably a fifth or sixth or seventh generation college student attending and the parents have the contacts to open doors for them. They have support systems, and what they don't have…their money can buy. Our students have nothing except the dreams and aspirations to make it some kind of way."

What do you feel are the strengths of JSU, and what impact have they had regarding your desegregation experience?

This researcher then pursued some more positive issues relative to JSU. Three senior-level administrators were asked what the strengths of the institution were. One administrator stated, "All you've got to do is look at the alumni record. We have produced folks that were written off and given no chance to succeed at all. We have educated kids who have become lawyers, doctors, congressmen and corporate executives. Our strength is that we can take nothing and turn it into something with literally nothing. We don't have to constantly talk about our success in terms of black and white all the time, because

I have counseled and advised them all. Nobody talks to Mississippi State about their success in black and white. I just keep this in mind: that children are not dumb because of their color. They are poorly skilled when they come because they didn't get the right training and nobody took the time to work with them. But if you look at us now since the last 30 years, we have gotten stronger in offering a variety of degrees, programs and services nobody would have imagined a few years ago. We've got nursing and business departments offering degrees. And we can do more if we get more money and more resources that we need."

Another administrator commented, "Jackson State University is one of the top-level doctoral-producing HBCUs. We are in the top 15 nationally and that ain't bad. You know what I mean? We've got some of the most advanced technology that Mississippi can offer. Did you know we got some of the most advanced computers and software allocated by the state? Did you know we've got fiber-optic cabling and INFER, which promotes collaboration between Mississippi's public school districts and other agencies to make sure we are providing academic, social and cultural services to everybody? Look, our test scores have gone up. Seventy-five percent of our students are passing the NTE (National Teacher Examination), and I know white schools that can't do that. We have more students graduating now than ever before. We've been able to attract white students and non-traditional students in increasing numbers at a faster rate than some of our white institutions who seek minority students of color. And we all get along. You don't hear about racism over here. We prove that you can get a good education with different people, different colors and different cultures. Did you read about how we got practical programs that make a difference? We got the Homeownership Opportunities Program (HOOP) and folks are getting community development, homes and improving their neighborhoods. I don't care what they say. We are being effective whether you are black or white. They've just got to stop looking at us in terms of just numbers. We are people, and we have experiences that others can learn from. We beat the odds with little or no financial assistance and support systems. Why doesn't anybody think that is important?"

Another senior-level administrator responded to the question about JSU strengths by mentioning, "I know for a fact that we graduated over 1,000 students in the last two years. You don't find those kinds of numbers too much with other HBCUs and TWIs in the state. For the last 10 years, JSU has placed in the top 16 when it comes to academic scholarships offered by private corporations like Honda. We offer international programs that diversify our curriculum and instructional process. We are now offering studies that students can't get at other institutions including Ole Miss. They have to come to JSU because we deliberately planned to offer things others couldn't because we are determined to be a university for all students. If you got the money, we've got the programs. Hey, in 10 years, JSU is going to be a melting pot with a little bit of everything for everybody. And that's something you bet we are proud of."

Further noted from this researcher's interview discussions with the gate-keepers was that the integrationists are pushing to keep Jackson State viable for the twenty-first century as a premier institution identical to Mississippi TWIs but with a significant characteristic of color that allows both races to peacefully and mutually co-exist. Although they represent roughly 30% of the administration and staff, according to the chief of staff and the director of institutional research, their views are not equally shared on campus or among their colleagues at other Mississippi institutions.

Theme Two: Towards a Historical Racially Identifiable Existence

Those opposed to Jackson State University's desegregation are called "anti-integrationists." They compromise approximately 30% of the administration and staff according to the chief of staff's view and reflect and reveal a bitter opinion of hurt, pain and unresolved desegregation issues. Accordingly, their views are that no amount of money can compensate for the oppression of Jackson State University. The Supreme Court's ruling was only a drop in the bucket of what was owed to Jackson State University and the state essentially is "getting off when it comes to providing equality in education in terms of academics and funding. At the heart of the anti-integrationists is the view that Jackson State University should not compromise its history or its future. Jackson State University should continue to be the vanguard of African-American history in Mississippi. The institution has a commitment and a sacred conviction to maintain its original purpose to educate people of color, this is why it was created and has been perpetuated through the years.

Interestingly, during this research on the impact of desegregation on Jackson State University, the opportunity to ask additional questions arose from among five entry-level administrators and staff who deal directly with the public day to day. This part of the interview process was initiated by recalling several of the before-mentioned success stories, records and accomplishments reported by the integrationists.

With those comments in mind, these employees were asked a series of questions about JSU and its strengths, public image, mission and desegregation impact as well as its challenges and obstacles in terms of student retention, etc. Many of the interviewees collectively agreed about the successes and achievements; however, one staff member said "Look, not everybody is going to tell you the good and the bad just because you are asking. A lot of folks don't want their names mentioned, and there are some of us who can't wait to tell anybody who will listen what the real deal is. Let me put his way, JSU needs to get real. We need to fight for everything we can get and keep everything we already have and more. I keep trying to tell these people here you cannot ignore or deny the real problems that jeopardize everything about the university

What obstacles, barriers and challenges has JSU had to overcome and/or may still be unresolved?

Another staff employee began to talk about her first year working at Jackson State University. She elaborated that she was now in her twelfth year and wonders why she has stayed this long. "The obstacles and the hell the state have put us through, I can't even begin to tell you all of it. They messed us up and then screwed us. Hell, they are still screwing us. We are supposed to be happy with $300 million, and they owed us $3 billion. Where's the justice in all of that? You know, let me ask you a question. How would you feel if you are constantly told to get and keep quality students but you can't give them full-paid scholarships, room and board? We were supposed to get upgraded computer systems to better run the school and we are still waiting. We had to wait for the Internet access, and then we were told you were getting this and you weren't getting that. We were the laughingstock of the state in some areas."

Another employee, an academic support services staff member and 13-year veteran talked about the challenges and barriers desegregation brought on when she stated, "It's been a bitch. You name it, and it's been a motherf_____ nightmare. The only time we could get real help and support to make sure our students got tutorial assistance, academic advisement and counseling was when we made it clear how many white students were going to benefit from it. And every time we bring on more white students, the less black we get. When did it ever become so bad to be black? We have a damn good history, and we need to keep our history. Hell, this is why most of our black students come here. They have been in all-white schools and all-white classes learning about all-white culture. How in the hell can you have strong self-esteem and be confident in who you are if all you know is white? I can't act white. I'm black. Tell somebody white to act black for a day. That doesn't make any damn sense. What makes us unique is our blackness. We (JSU) make African-Americans feel loved, supported and confident, and that they can achieve in a strong black environment. When they see professionals that look like them and talk like them, it makes them feel good about themselves. You can't get that at a white institution. The white administrators and faculty are not going to get personal with you where you feel comfortable. They can't even relate. How are we going to keep what has made us strong if we keep becoming less black and more white? And why do we have to apologize for being black? Nobody white is apologizing for being white. Look, I'm just trying to tell you that the more we adopt their goals (the white colleges and universities), the more we lose a little bit of who we are and what brought us this far. It ain't fair. They (whites) get the money. They get the best equipment, they get the scholarships, they get the buildings and we get whatever is left over…if there is anything left over. And then we have to wait forever to get it. It's not like we get it next week. It's years, and then we are supposed to be happy. Those are your barriers. Those are your obstacles. And if you ask me, the state needs to remove it because they put us in this mess."

Another staff member working in the Division of Student Life commented, "I support the president and all that he is doing. He's a great guy, and I like him and I know he means well. But you know, they got his hands tied. They want him to lead us into being more white and less black to the point where color won't ever matter. I don't agree with that. That's wrong. The judge made me mad when he said we have to become less black and more white. You didn't hear anybody telling the University of Southern Mississippi, the Mississippi University for Women and Delta State to become less white and more multi-racial. I guess my point is this: We don't have to stop being black in order to be academically above the standards."

After hearing these interviewees comment about another side of Jackson State University, this researcher was able to feel and to see other issues and perceptions that existed regarding their desegregation experience. In many ways, the perceptions of these anti-integrationists are unheard of in the eye of the public.

The anti-integrationists are simply arguing that diversifying Jackson State University means less black programs, less black faculty, less black students, less black culture and less black graduations. The questions they pose include: (a) Why does Jackson State University have to be the one to change and change more than others (TWIs in Mississippi)? (b) Why should Jackson State University have to sacrifice and suffer for the racist policies, perceptions and treatment inflicted upon it for trying to being equal? The anti-integrationists want to see Jackson State University stay the way it has been in terms of black culture, socialization, activities, programs and events, but this time with the state's money it was owed. The anti-integrationists believe to compromise is to hand the institution over to the state and the eventual demise of this once proud of HBCU. Although the student retention rate is poor and Jackson State University has struggled with limited funds, this camp is strongly committed to self-determination regardless of the statistics. Jackson State University's own self-study that is consistent with the SACS Accreditation Report Annual Report, 2002, justifies their position. For the anti-integrationists, the record is that despite the lack of funding equity from the State of Mississippi:

1. JSU is in full compliance with all SACS criteria.
2. Academic/non-academic units mission goals and records are consistent with the institution.
3. Financial, physical and human resources enable them to fulfill the institution's mission.
4. Instructional support services in all academic schools are diverse and are adequately addressing the deficiencies of the institution. They will in time consistently exceed the academic expectations and requirements by the state.
5. Research advancements have been made in major areas, thus resulting in increased state funding and allocations.
6. Milestones have been reached in terms of international programs along with new programs in allied health sciences, engineering and social work.
7. Jackson State University is a comprehensive, co-educational, public institution that continuously produces the majority of African-American degree recipients with bachelor's, master's, specialist's and doctoral degrees in Mississippi; it is ranked in the top 15 HBCUs for producing African-American doctoral degree recipients.
8. Jackson State University, while maintaining its African-American base student population and academic success via administrators, faculty and student graduates, has achieved the highest approval and attainable accreditation level with SACS-Level VI. Therefore it must be doing something right and institutionally effective.

Further, the anti-integrationists argue that the president hasn't gone far enough to ensure the security of African-American history, culture and preservation of black contributions presently and for the future. They insist that the burden remains forever on the State of Mississippi to adequately fund and support them academically with adequate resources, programs, technology and support systems to ensure its survival. This camp is outspoken, aggressive and determined to define Jackson State as the premier institution to preserve and perpetuate African-American survival in Mississippi. The anti-integrationists further articulate the need for more multi-cultural and ethnically based activities as well as programs to cultivate an atmosphere of support and comfort to its constituents. Their opposition is to the president's vision of being nonracially identifiable, because it is viewed as a concession to the state that desires to dismantle Jackson State University as a predominantly African-American institution perpetuating black culture and academic success.

How would you describe Jackson State University's relationship with the Council on Higher Learning and the state legislature in general and over the years?

This researcher was able to ask further questions about JSU's internal perceptions regarding how some felt about their relationship with the Council on Higher Learning and the State Legislature. Three senior-level administrators were eager to comment on this question because they had had several years of interaction with the state through task force assignments from the university. One administrator stated, "No matter how you look at it and how the media reports it, the Council and the State Legislature see us as a 'thorn' in their side. We just won't go away, and they have tried every conceivable strategy to ignore us, evade us and elude us when it comes to our issues. Everything we do is political. But you have to understand they are the 'political machine.' If you upset them or don't approach them the right way, then it's going to be a long dry summer. They can be trifling in subtle ways. They sit on measures and delay making decisions that could impact us financially by running everything through their own sub-committees. We are forever waiting and debating and dialoguing and disagreeing. Sometimes I don't even know how we ever made it this far."

Another administrator stated, "It's a 'paternalistic' relationship. We are still down South and it takes generations to change attitudes and habits and behaviors. If you don't interact with people of color and if you don't talk with us, you end up talking at us. The bottom line is that we are treated like we are 'field niggers' on a plantation on some issues and 'house niggers' on other issues. They don't come out and say it, but it's in their attitude, their tones and their discussions. The only difference is now they don't call me 'boy,' they just call me 'Jim' or 'Charlie.' And they think that's progress and that there is nothing wrong. The key to keeping us (JSU) in check is the 'executive session' discussions. It's when they go into their own private discussions and dialogue out of the eyes and the ears of the public. They then come back with decisions as to who, what, when, where and why or they table it. But you never get a real sense of why and what really went on or where their minds were heading and what we can do to enhance the relationship. We are not opposed to whites coming to our campus, but we are opposed to them making us less black so they can feel more comfortable. And it's crazy, because I never read it and I never head it ever mentioned that anyone was ever concerned about if blacks were comfortable at TWIs. That's why we have to have a black university, so our people can feel comfortable. If you feel comfortable you can achieve."

A third administrator said "I'll explain it this way and you can do the math. They are bureaucrats with venom. We (JSU) are the rats and the campus is the cage. This is why we have to stay black, because whenever they show up or get involved with us, somebody has to die. There are casualties at this institution every year because somebody's politics weren't good. We've got spies and traitors among us. You can't trust anybody here. The only people who are not aware of this completely are the students who come here. And maybe they don't need to know how bad it really is because if they do, the State will have their head on a platter."

Why do students choose Jackson State University vs. a TWI in Mississippi?

This researcher then turned to issues dealing with students and the impact of desegregation at Jackson State University.

Several mid-level administrators and support staff were adamant about who attends JSU. For those discussing this issue, it was something that gave them a foundation to justify Jackson State University's existence and success. "We have to stay black because this institution is really all that we have and nobody wants to send their kids out of state and pay out all that money somewhere else," commented a secretary.

A recruitment administrator further added that she was proud of those who came to JSU and why they came. "Look, our students are so diverse and so different in terms of their aspirations. They come because of our reputation. They come because their family members went here. And all they are doing is following tradition. Some come to JSU because they know there are good black faculty and programs here. The tuition is affordable and that makes a big difference. Nobody is going to go where they can't really afford it. And you can't overlook the fact that most of the time either they know somebody that is here or went here, or they are coming because their high school friends are coming."

At this point during in conversation with this interviewee, this researcher inquired about the negatives regarding why students don't attend JSU. An employee who specializes in financial aid and admissions commented, "Yes, we do run into image problems and credibility problems because there are a lot of folks out there that think if you get your degree from an HBCU then it is less credible. There are others who feel like we can't teach them as well as a TWI or we can't give them enough money for them to make it through all four years to get their degrees. They have heard about other HBCUs struggling with no money so they are scared to try us. But we show them the facts about the financial aid we have offered over the years. We also talk to them about how they ought to come because their chances of success are just as good here as anywhere else. They are informed that half of all black doctors and lawyers and educators got their undergraduate degrees from HBCUs. That it's not only what you know but also who you know. Those who make it come back to our campus to visit and to advise and help others. We try to get them to understand that when you stand before a corporate executive you've still got to know your stuff no matter where your degree came from. That white school's name may get you in, but you've still got to produce and JSU has graduates that produce. We compete just as well as anybody else."

Another support staff person in the Office of Records and Registration gave her views and perceptions on the desegregation impact and why students still came to JSU. For her, they come because they are tired of the racism and the attitudes they get from whites. They come also because they know it's a different world being around mostly blacks. HBCUs are good because we don't espouse racism and hatred; we just simply appreciate being black. You don't lose high standards and quality learning just because of color. And somebody needs to be saying more about this.

Anti-integrationists further believe that white Mississippians should have access to Jackson State University but that the institution should maintain its "African-American experiences and culture that can't be found elsewhere at white institutions."

What do you feel is the future role of Jackson State University?

One support specialist expressed her fear that the future role of Jackson State University was not clear to her. "We're not going anywhere and they are going to have to deal with us. We will do what we have always done. We will be the black 'flagship' school of the state. We will find a way to help blacks mainly and whoever else to achieve and to become that doctor, that lawyer, that engineer, that nurse or that judge."

Another staff employee, a secretary, stated that our mission is supposed to be meeting the needs of African-Americans in Mississippi. Well, we are doing it. The Court is not going to change that. They know we are not going to go anywhere. They know we are not happy being at the white institutions and the whites are not going to come here unless they can't go anywhere else. So, we just do what have been doing. We've been educating and training folks to be professionals in their chosen field. I don't get to say nothing at these meetings, but I listen to them a lot. And I can tell you right now, Jackson State University is going to be a teacher's college, an engineering school, a graduate school and whatever else we can get. All we got to do is make sure we are putting out the numbers and the state is getting its money's worth for each student that shows up."

A senior-level administrator said, "Our role is constantly changing. Hopefully we are going to still be black. They might get rid of MVSU and Alcorn, but they are not going to get rid of us. You've got to remember a few years ago we only trained teachers and social workers. A few years after that we trained business entrepreneurs and engineers. Our role is to find those occupations for the future and lobby the state to allow us to teach them and train students in them. But we cannot diminish the number of blacks we need to push through those programs. I'm just afraid that we will end up getting a whole bunch of white students and the black students won't take advantage of these opportunities. The court litigation has just made a lot of us fight to keep what we already have and make others take for granted what we could get out of this whole situation. When we see more whites showing up, we know something is up. The question is simply where are the people of color in these programs? Because if we lose our history and culture and color, then Jackson State University is gone. But you know how that is. Not everybody believes we need to stay black, but all I can say is they need to 'wake up and smell the coffee.'"

Theme Three: Towards Both a Racially Identifiable and A Non-Racially Identifiable Existence

This researcher explored other views on campus by contacting several mid- and entry-level employees who offered other intriguing perceptions about Jackson State University. These gatekeepers have spent considerable time at the institution, ranging from 10-20 years, primarily holding the same position. They have seen generations of students come and go during this time and had several comments to offer. This third and equally compelling camp affected by the impact of desegregation revealed that there is yet another major set of perceptions that exists unobtrusively at Jackson State University.

Composed of primarily lower-and mid-level administrators and staff, their views take the position that is often seen and heard as less vocal and less obvious to the public. Essentially, they are neutral in that they do not outwardly embrace the new direction to enhance and expand Jackson State University under its current leadership. Further, they are not completely comfortable or convinced that Jackson State University can ultimately safeguard its own black heritage for the future. The neutralists are the administrators and staff members who want advancement but at a slow rate and route without the compromise of becoming exclusively or less black. Their Achilles heel is that they lack the power and political influence to mandate change and provide a bargaining position that poses a threat of continuous pressure.

The neutralists simply carry out the day-to-day operations. Their job titles and positions are primarily custodian, service worker, secretary, specialist, entry-level administrator and junior faculty. A small percentage of tenured faculty, estimated at 20% (Okoye, 2003), holds this perception and position at Jackson State University. This researcher was referred to a few of these employees by the chief of staff after following up on other contacts with senior-level administrators. One of the first questions that these employees were asked dealt with their perception of Jackson University in terms of its image, mission and goals. Secondly, they were asked whether or not they felt the institution was adequately serving its purpose.

What do you feel is the perception of Jackson State University publicly and privately?

One entry-level service worker stated that his perception of JSU was that it was great institution that gave a lot of help to a lot of people. He further commented, "You can just tell that a lot of people that come through here are better when they leave. They learn and they grow and they experience things they couldn't get anywhere else. Everybody I know feels good about us."

Another employee who works in mid-level management responded to the question by stating, "We are loved by the black community and viewed as suspect by the white community. We can never do enough to make them feel comfortable and acceptable."

Two staff secretaries in the College of Arts and Sciences stated that they really don't know enough about what really goes down and what is really at stake until after the fact. As one secretary put it, "We hear stuff. You know, the rumors, the gossip, the innuendoes and all of that. But then some of it happens and some of it doesn't happen. We will just be glad when they give us the money and let us do what we need to do. We are all right the way we are, but we know we could improve in a lot of areas. And that means we have to bring in more whites, because you know the white folks are not going to have anything second class. I want us to keep our black heritage, but you can't say that too loud around here. I know a girl who lost her job because she kept complaining about becoming too white. I guess they got tired of hearing it."

An employee who spends all his time conducting research for the university voiced his concerns by saying, "We have to take it slow. Everybody wants change and they want it now. But that is not going to happen. We have to be held accountable and make sure we take care of business. Nobody is going to give you money and facilities if they don't trust you. The way I see it, we can be both black and white and not lose anything."

Further, this researcher found probably some of the most profound statements made by a facilities management employee who said that the institution's image was great on campus but that the white public always has something to criticize us about. She added, "What gets me is nobody wants to know what we think and how we feel. All they want is for us to keep the wheels oiled and turning. We support the president, and we support our history. The problem is that white people think those two views are mutually exclusive."

Another employee, a grounds and landscape worker, stated, "We are trying not to make too much noise over this thing because the louder we complain or protest, the more we run risks. We just need to let this thing blow over. You know, sometimes you can get more done by not saying anything at all. At least not too loud."

Obvious at this point was the fact that, for many employees, Jackson State University was fulfilling its state-mandated mission and being institutionally effective. Their concern was more about surviving the impact and the desegregation process in terms of job security and reorganization.

The neutralists have survived because they are non-confrontational, but with opinions. They view the impact of desegregation as both painful and positive. The financial impact will increase their salaries and resources to be effective and efficient; however, they fear the loss of control through possible reorganization and strategic planning that may not include them for the future. A consistent complaint articulated by this group is their concern that they are between the crossroads of progress and maintaining a past of rich black history and heritage. Yet, they offer very few suggestions and recommendations on how to survive. Their perception is that the top-level administrators and the state legislators will ultimately win with their agenda because they have the power, the politics and the financial resources to implement change. The members of this camp also see themselves as simply the fieldworkers who get the job done but have little influence over what should be done.

Who supports and who does not support the president's vision, leadership and direction?

In response to this question, a senior-level administrator stated, "It's hard to tell who supports the president and who doesn't. So many people talk out both sides of their mouth. There are few who speak their minds and don't mind telling others, but we've got a lot of people who just think its best to keep your real thoughts to yourself until you leave campus. Hey, nobody wants to rock the boat. We didn't want anybody to be blamed if we didn't get a settlement."

Another employee, a mid-level administrator, said "We don't know how far we have to go and keep going to be white enough and how far we have to go and keep going to stay black enough. It's like trying to please everybody, and you know you just can't do that all the time. Somebody is going to lose. And if you ask me, JSU has lost too many times and too much already."

A support specialist commented, "It doesn't matter who supports the president, his vision and his direction too much because sooner or later we all have to make sure we don't come across as a bunch of 'Negroes' with a lot of money over here having a party with white people's money."

An office staff employee in the School of Education commented, 'This mess (this desegregation thing) is never really over. Somebody is always checking and rechecking to make sure we stay in our place. So we have to end up walking a thin line and skating on ice. I sort of feel like we can keep our history and yet become bigger, better and more inclusive without losing anything. But we don't worry too much about it, because after it is all said and done and the dust has cleared, we know that black people want to be around black people and white people want to be around white people."

Two mid-level academic support service employees had further comments to add. One stated, "We can become more white by day and less black at night or we can be more black by day and less white at night."

Another specialist commented that the goal is to bridge two worlds (one black and one white) and to bridge two directions (staying black enough and yet embracing their culture). "We know we need leadership that will help us keep what we have and yet give us something new. It's just a new day up in here and everybody has to get real. We got the money although we should have gotten more. And we have to make do with what we have for now and hope we get more later. But it won't be easy. My only problem is we have so much stuff that we still haven't corrected, cleaned up and addressed. The state hasn't addressed anything, if you ask me. They want us to compete with Ole Miss and Southern Miss academically, but we can't get finances, support systems, the best instructors, the best facilities and buildings and then they don't pay anybody anything.

You see all of this has not been solved or resolved. They just sort left us hanging. Either direction we pick we are wrong, and they jump on us so we do what we got to do."

Based on these comments, it became clear to this researcher that these neutralist gatekeepers are caught between two worlds. They are not firmly committed to the new leadership, but they are not convinced they can maintain the "black" Jackson State University they once knew and experienced before the desegregation litigation. The neutralists express frustration and disappointment as well because they see Jackson State University as an institution with too many compromisers and not enough aggressive fighters to validate its importance, black success and contributions. Their perceptions are further reflected through the view that "change means loss of power and control." Subsequently, they feel further excluded and alienated from the climate and culture that once cultivated African-American higher learning in Mississippi.

Their perceptions also reveal anxiety and animosity over the "whitening of the campus" and the threat of less blackness than there once was. What is also intriguing is that the neutralists see the impact of desegregation as a "win-lose" dilemma. Jackson State University wins with the reception of long-awaited finances but loses in terms of color and campus climate, because the fear is it cannot maintain over the long run a dominant black culture pre-eminent in Mississippi. And for many, this fear is apparently an issue to be addressed by future generations.

Summary Interview Interpretations and Findings

From the before-mentioned views expressed by three equally important and distinct social perceptions held at Jackson State University, it is apparent that this institution is challenged to find common ground. The impact of desegregation has left both a challenge and a climate of change in many respects for the good and possibly the not so good. Jackson State University is internally proud of its many accomplishments. Its graduates have gone on to assume roles in corporate boardrooms, law firms, medicine and the sciences. The institution has achieved nationally and regionally recognized milestones in teaching, research, service and technology.

Jackson State University's self-study report clearly boasts of its graduates performing outstanding work in major fields. These successes are far too many to mention in detail. Students who have had deficient academic preparation have overcome great odds and achieved outstanding success in the real world. If it had not been for Jackson State University, these students may have not become contributing citizens to society in positive, productive and proactive ways. Jackson State University's gatekeepers are further convinced that their school serves a vital and strategic purpose in the lives of all Mississippians, especially African-Americans, because of its past experiences and accomplishments as well as the opportunities it has provided academically, professionally and community-wise.

Conversely, there are troubling signs of an institution that is unable to shake the ghost of the past because of vestiges of racism in terms of attitudes and behaviors that persist. Although the black-white relationships have significantly improved relative to communication, social interactions and mutual learning, Jackson State University has yet to confidently convince a larger statewide community that its white residents are just as welcomed (as its black students) to a world of higher education that ensures safety, stability, support and success. This dilemma may not entirely be Jackson State University's problem. The acquisition of higher education is predicated mainly on the basis of choice. African-Americans choose to attend Jackson State University for reasons and experiences that they cannot always successfully acquire at TWIs. White Americans choose to attend Jackson State University because of cost efficiency, convenient location and accessibility as well as state-based professional development programs and opportunities. White students at this institution are far more likely to be non-traditional: they are not the typical 18 to 22-year-old college student. They are more likely to be better focused, more mature, older, more advanced professionally and more economically stable. Further, their experiences at Jackson State University usually mean attending classes and having little or no social interaction with the predominantly black student population.

JSU may literally be doing all that it can do to attract and retain a greater white Mississippi student population. This institution is further challenged to address many unresolved issues and questions that threaten its stability and clarify its role for the twenty-first century. Given such a reality, a number of unresolved issues were revealed from the interviews with gatekeepers at Jackson State University. Many of these issues, which remain both complex and controversial, cannot be overlooked or ignored and apparently are unresolved at this point.

1. Many students enter but do not graduate.

2. JSU produces only 19. 4% of African-American graduates while MVSU has a graduation rate of 66.8%.

3. The State of Mississippi invests in its citizens through higher education by allocating specific amounts of monies per full-time-equivalent stu-

dent. The success of the institution in terms of graduation rates appears to indicate the state actually loses money and does not receive adequate return on its investment in many African-American students at JSU.

4. The deterioration of JSU's physical facilities (due to the lack of state funding) unquestionably impacts student attendance, retention and success versus TWIs in Mississippi.

5. Would JSU actually have greater institutional effectiveness in terms of degree completions, enrollment, instructional programs, graduation rates and mission assignments if it were better funded to implement programs, resources, support services and upgraded facilities?

6. Jackson State University has less paid faculty in comparison to TWIs in the state. Less paid faculty may indicate that JSU and other HBCUs in Mississippi may attract less qualified faculty in terms of degrees, experience, research and publications, etc., versus higher-paying institutions. The quality of learning may be in jeopardy. Further, the ability to attract the brightest and the most contributing faculty with outstanding track records of excellence is directly tied to compensation.

7. On the average, students who enter JSU are significantly less academically prepared for college and experience higher risk factors that impact their retention. Jackson State University may be losing students through no internal fault but through external factors beyond its control: limited or nonexistent domestic support systems, insufficient family financial assistance, unclear college expectations, on-campus institutional and environmental alienation, etc.

8. JSU, like the two other HBCUs in Mississippi, appears to be historically more mal-nourished than TWIs, thus they may lose quality faculty, students and programs.

9. How much desegregation is enough for JSU in terms of racial composition, facilities and programs offered?

10. Is the State of Mississippi's relationship with JSU simply a paternalistic one? The public and private images of Jackson State University are clearly defined along racial lines; therefore, its mission may or may not be hindered. Ultimately, questions arise that ask what have we learned through this desegregation process at one HBCU, Jackson State University. What are the benefits of the desegregation of Jackson State University? Is there a sociological benefit inclusive/exclusive of race for students to attend an HBCU, specifically Jackson State University? The social perceptions at Jackson State University reveal a continued lack of

trust and faith in a predominantly white higher education system from its inception. Such perceptions and feelings appear indicative of Mississippi's long struggle for racial equality. If Mississippians are still struggling with economic, political, residential and community equality, it stands to reason that such elements have permeated the walls of higher education. Further, this study sheds light on the existence of a historical truth that Jackson State University is unable to completely and exclusively define its role and mission as in the past on its own terms without heavy causalities and conflict with external forces.

This study forces Mississippians (white and black) to confront the reality that to be predominantly black does not necessarily mean to be "anti-white." Jackson State University's historical co-existence with TWIs in Mississippi to the present day proves that institutions can exist and serve distinct colors, cultures and citizens' needs and that it is possible and practical to peacefully co-exist with limited conflict and serve any person who desires a higher education. Also revealed by the study is that the social perceptions of the impact of desegregation (whether good or bad) will not necessarily result in positive reception or implementation.

The perceptions expressed through the interviews also convey that institutional effectiveness is measurable in both quantitative and qualitative terms. There is an urgency to value and consider the attitudes, feelings, emotions and experiences of those who foster learning to diverse populations. Social perceptions also tell a side of the desegregation equation that may not be quantitatively measurable in terms of morale, motivation, feelings and the means by which to define a clear role by those who implement change. These perceptions reveal that integration cannot necessarily be forced or eliminated because of the reality of freedom of choice among the constituents desiring a higher education.

One clear conclusion or inference that can be drawn from this study is that the definitive reality that Jackson State University's mission for the twenty-first century is to continue to serve two important roles: (a) to provide quality education through degrees and programs offered to a primarily African-American population for which it has done in the past, and (b) to chart its future course to include non-African-Americans on a limited basis through programs and services germane to a specific white Mississippi population. These programs may be more highly specialized, technological and more consumer-oriented than before.

What cannot be clearly determined from the impact of desegregation on this institution is to what extent and in what context all the roles and responsibilities of Jackson State University will have for this century. Numerous variables, including politics; state funding; and the ever-changing demographics of the state in terms of race, gender, age and residence complicate specific plans that will remain permanent but subject to adaptations and adjustments by both the state and the institution itself. My guess is that JSU's role will be the same as in the past. It will continue to educate the vast majority of African-Americans with no more than a 20% increase in white students; it will continue to be the vanguard of black history in Mississippi.

Further analysis and inference can be drawn from the interviews with the three major camps impacted by desegregation to conclude that Jackson State University has a choice and a chance to advance itself through technology and other resources to be on the cutting edge of educating and equipping not only African-Americans but also white Americans in Mississippi in ways it has never done before. Jackson State University must do now and in the future what it has done in the past: educate disadvantaged, underrepresented and disenfranchised minority populations in Mississippi (IHL Report, 2002).

The data reveal that African-Americans are far more successful in achieving a higher education at Jackson State University that results in a degree and training than those African-Americans who have attended Mississippi's TWIs. African-American students who attend Jackson State University do so for a number of reasons:

1. The school has a good reputation.
2. The school offers a generous financial aid package.
3. The school has course offerings unique to the interests of African-Americans
4. and these are taught by a significant number of African-Americans.
5. The administrators, faculty, staff and specialists who run Jackson State University serve as immediate and personal role models for aspiring students.
6. The parents and guardians to students have a favorable perception or previous experience or previous exposure with Jackson State University that may or may not include graduation.
7. The parents and guardians of the African-American students are more likely to have attended Jackson State University.
8. Students believe they have just as good a chance, if not better, towards acquiring gainful employment with a degree from Jackson State University than from earning one at a Mississippi TWI.
9. African-American students who attend Jackson State University feel academically supported, socially accepted and personally invested in by the

administrators, faculty and staff, thus increasing their motivation to succeed at the collegiate level.

10. The tuition is cost-efficient or lower than Mississippi's TWIs.

11. The cost of living in the area is relatively inexpensive.

12. African-American students who attend usually have friends and/or family members who are also attending, thus giving rise to an immediate and familiar support system and shared sense of cohesiveness.

13. Students have a flexible option to work and go to school as well as socialize with other African-Americans who migrate from in state, out of state and foreign countries.

14. Students feel they have a better option to work, go to school and maintain residence and ties to their homes in the immediate community or region. Jackson State University is accessible with less sacrifices and obstacles to immediately overcome.

15. Students feel the university is successful in job placement and preparing students for advanced graduate education.

16. Students feel they are academically challenged with less pressure and less racism to encounter.

17. Students and community residents actually identify with Jackson State University as a safe and strategic haven to perpetuate black culture, black values and black self-esteem.

Further, Jackson State University's identity is tied to its mission of being a historically black, co-educational, research-intensive public urban institution of higher learning. Desegregation has not diminished this historical role or responsibility. Jackson State continues to have a specific mission to implement new growth, new direction, new course offerings, new programs and new services to its constituents that were once only offered through Mississippi's TWIs. But this time, the focus should be to provide specific educational programs in areas underrepresented by minorities, such as the sciences, business, engineering and healthcare, etc. The institution still has a role and responsibility to train, develop and utilize human, cultural and physical resources to address the needs of its surrounding metropolitan urban communities. Jackson State University also has the role of addressing major issues that affect other urban areas of Mississippi statewide. By keeping with its current and past mission, Jackson State University can build on what it has done effectively in the past…address the needs of a primarily African-American population in Mississippi. It also opens its arms to new horizons and an increased white population.

CHAPTER FIVE

Conclusions and Overview

This study examined the impact of desegregation on one HBCU, Jackson State University in terms of (a) the performance indicators that actually measure institutional effectiveness, and (b) the internal perceptions of selective leaders at the institution through personal interviews. Both measures were done with the effort to address the *Fordice* ruling and establish if there was any justification for the continued existence or discontinuance of Jackson State University.

Since the advent of desegregation legislation designed to provide access and opportunity for African-Americans to attend historically white institutions brought scrutiny and suspicion regarding the status and continuing need of HBCUs, two camps or philosophical viewpoints emerged, fueling a debate. Those that promote the continuation of the HBCU have argued that these institutions fulfill a unique role and offer a wealth of evidence and track record to suggest continuation. Those who oppose the HBCUs suggest that a racially based school for the African-American student is no longer needed because all schools are now open and freely accessible to black, white and foreign students alike.

The original research question asked was, "What evidence exists to justify the continued existence or the discontinuance of HBCUs, specifically Jackson State University?" A related question included, "What has been the impact of desegregation on one particular HBCU, Jackson State University, in terms of institutional effectiveness relating to specific key performance indicators?"

Additional questions ensuing from these initial questions were: (a) Where should HBCUs exist? (b) If so, in what context(s)? (c) What kind of education should an HBCU provide in the twenty-first century? (d) How should the HBCU relate to the dominant political, economic and social environment that prevails in U.S. society? (e) Is there a sociological benefit to students attending an HBCU in terms of academics, culture and achievement?

After completing and analyzing the quantitative and qualitative data obtained through this study, several major conclusions and recommendations for further research have been generated. The purpose of this chapter is to first elaborate on HBCUs, and Jackson State University in particular, in terms of having an existence tied to the dominant social, economic and political environment of America. Secondly, to demonstrate that Jackson State University, and HBCUs in general, have strong sociological benefits to their constituents. Thirdly, to discuss this researcher's conclusion or position that HBCUs in general and Jackson State University in particular, have an educationally justified basis for their continued existence. And finally, to provide some general overall conclusions and specific recommendations so that there is a clear understanding about any justifiable evidence as to whether or not to continue or discontinue Jackson State University in light of *Fordice*. If there is, what will be Jackson State University's continuing role in serving the state of Mississippi and its citizens? How can it achieve and maintain its role? What possible areas of further research should be explored in the coming years to address any justifiable evidence to continue Jackson State University and other HBCUs?

The Relationship of HBCUs to the Dominant Social, Economic and Political Environment of America

The findings of this study show that there is clearly a relationship between HBCUs and the dominant social, economic and political environment of America. In a longitudinal study titled, "The Shape of the River: Long-Term Consequences of Considering Race in College and University Admissions," by William Bowen and Derek Bok, 1976 and 1989 cohorts of students were studied from selective colleges and universities. In looking specifically at HBCUs, Bowen and Bok found that most African-Americans (like those at TWIs) who were admitted to these institutions under affirmative-action policies succeeded in college, established careers and assumed major leadership roles in their communities at a higher rate. The leadership roles were not uncommonly found to be in banking, social services, local city politics, healthcare, community action agencies and community economic empowerment programs. Equally important, underrepresented students (minorities) who attended HBCUs were four times more likely than other graduates to actually practice medicine, business entrepreneurial activities and politics in "socio-economically deprived" areas (Bowen, 1998). According to a report presented at the Annual Symposium and Working Research Meeting on Diversity and Affirmative Action in 1999:

If African-American and Latino workers were represented at colleges and universities in the same proportion as their share of 18-to-24 year-olds, the U.S. wealth would increase $231 billion every year, annual tax revenues would increase by $80 billion and the proportion of minority families with inadequate incomes would decrease (Carnevale, 1999, p. 17). Further noted was the value of HBCUs in citing that if the African-American and Latino "...communities had the same distribution of college education as non-Hispanic white communities, it would help ensure an adequate supply of skilled workers that is currently absent in the workforce" (p. 17). Implicit in this finding is the reality that there is a continued need to prepare diverse students on our college campuses. Jackson State University and other HBCUs, have a continuing vital and significant role to play in ensuring these results for the twenty-first century. They do so because HBCUs are the symbols and practical applications of institutions that provide diversity and multicultural experiences indicative of an ever-increasingly diverse world. Indeed, it is in such multicultural environments that HBCUs do their transformation work by laying a foundation and fervor for minority students to contribute to society in terms of economics, politics and social change. These institutions have proved themselves capable of "...taking students who have received minimal, modest and inadequate secondary education or those whose aptitude was not through the traditional assessment methods (i.e., the SAT or ACT) and produced talented contributing citizens" (Gray, 2000, p. 9). Jackson State University, like so many other HBCUs, knows how to take diamonds in the rough and polish them to brilliance, like the Harvards and the Stanfords. But they also know how to do something other colleges cannot do. "They know how to take a lump of coal and turn it into a diamond" by mentoring, expecting excellence and hands-on teaching by faculty who have been there and care (Gray, 2000, p. 9).

The Sociological Benefits of Attending an HBCU

Not only do HBCUs successfully participate and effectively relate to the social, economic and political fabric of America, they also provide clear sociological benefits. This researcher initiated this study through careful and critical strategies intended to explore the origin, the history, the importance and the challenges that JSU and other HBCUs may face. Interwoven within this approach was the continuous assessment as to whether or not any social benefits were derived from attending an HBCU. As a result of such investigation, this researcher is firmly convinced that HBCUs serve a vital role in our society and should continue to do so. There is, without question, a sociological benefit to students (black or white) attending an HBCU. HBCUs are entities of diversity and multiculturalism. By emphasizing diversity as either a matter of institutional policy or in faculty research and teaching, JSU provides students with curricular and extracurricular opportunities for them to experience racial and multicultural issues associated with widespread effects on a student's cognitive and affective development (Astin, 1993). When one looks at the historical track record of these institutions in light of the great odds and obstacles they've encountered, one has to stop and pause to salute their incredible journey and successes.

Further, if one is to conduct a literature search or ask the average African-American college graduate of an HBCU why anyone should fight to save the historically black college and university, the findings are earth-shattering. First, according to statistics and despite the increase of blacks attending TWIs, HBCUs still continue to educate and graduate a substantial proportion of black youth. What continues to be a problem is the phenomenon known as a "revolving-door policy" which is in effect at white institutions. The minority attrition rate at TWIs nationally varies from 70% to 85% according to W.G. Smith (1976), author of *Diversity Works; The Emerging Picture of How Students Benefit* In 1976 black colleges graduated 20% to 25% of their student enrollment while white institutions graduated about 3% minority enrollment. Obviously, something is wrong.

Secondly, in spite of governmental complaints about fiduciary responsibility, black institutions continue to perpetuate their reputation for accomplishing more with less. When one looks at the fact that 75% of all black PhD's received their baccalaureate degrees from HBCUs, positive social change is clearly reflected. Also important to understand is that 80% of all black physicians, 90% of all black dentists, 75% of black military officers, 40% of all black physicists and astronomers, 60% of all high-level federal civil servants and 50% of all black public school teachers received their undergraduate degrees from an HBCU (Allen, 1991). Noteworthy, too, is the fact that HBCUs currently produce 30% of all postsecondary degrees to African-Americans. Moreover, students attending these schools were almost twice as likely to major in science and engineering as compared to minorities attending majority white institutions. It is conclusive that without HBCUs many young African-Americans and many working-class whites would never see the inside of a college classroom. While HBCUs make up only 3% of our nation's colleges and universities, they produce 28% of black undergraduate degrees (Allen, 1991).

The number of black students enrolled at HBCUs has now reached an all-time high. Figures compiled recently indicate more than 360,000 students were enrolled at HBCU, representing an increase of 26% over the last 18 years despite full financial-aid packages offered by competing TWIs (Henderson, 2003). The HBCUs are also vital because the typical 4-year HBCU serves as a gateway to graduate and professional-level schools. These so-called most liberal arts colleges and state-based institutions tend to offer more direct, accessible mentors and role models for students that result in African-American achievement and success.

There are yet additional sociological benefits, which are far-reaching beyond measure. White students and parents (especially those who are non-traditional and offspring of working class and impoverished backgrounds) are discovering what African-Americans have known for decades: that many HBCUs offer a quality education for about half the price of comparable mainstream schools. HBCUs also serve as training grounds for leadership roles and responsibilities among African-Americans. It is at an HBCU that the average black can be elected, appointed and serve as a president, secretary, treasurer, student government leader, advisor and specialist that in a majority institutional setting would not be reasonably achievable.

Another sociological benefit is what HBCUs contribute. What they have given to the social, economic and moral composition of American society is notable. Black colleges imbue their students with intangible realities like self-confidence, a sense of dignity and worth, faith in higher possibilities, belief in the future and viability, general optimism and self-projection, all of which are essential to the realization of the American dream. Sociologically speaking, these institutions stress cultural awareness, a black-on-black setting and the importance of black role models. They also seek to create cultures of difference rather than deprivation, to build skills and enhance self-awareness (Gurin, 2003). These qualities white American institutions either cannot or do not impart nearly as effectively to minority populations. This is a benefit that JSU and other HBCUs offer that many students of color either cannot and or do not obtain at TWIs.

A further asset seen at HBCUs is the ability of different races and cultures to interact, co-participate and socialize both in structured and non-structured environments. For example, it is at HBCUs that the successful social interaction between races occurs in intramural and intercollegiate activities. When TWIs and HBCUs compete against each other athletically, it also offers an opportunity for the public, students and athletes to intermingle, associate and develop long-standing relationships that often last long after the collegiate experience.

They also serve as instruments of affirmative action. The typical HBCU is at least 10% white in undergraduate student population and may actually exceed 50% of the student population on the graduate level. This finding is significant because: A racially and ethnically diverse university or student body has far-ranging and significant benefits for all students, non-minorities and minorities alike. Students learn better in a diverse educational environment, and they are better prepared to become active participants in our pluralistic, democratic society once they leave such a setting (Gurin, 2003, p. 4).

The findings in this study indicate that Jackson State University, like other HBCUs, strongly perpetuates diversity initiatives that impact student attitudes, feelings toward intergroup relations, institutional satisfaction, involvement, retention and academic growth. Like so many HBCUs, Jackson State University consistently produces students who convey feelings of positive institutional satisfaction, involvement and academic growth. What Jackson State University has done like so many other HBCUs is demonstrate that serious engagements in diversified curriculums and classrooms result in positive impact on attitudes toward racial issues. These institutions provide a microcosm of opportunities to interact in deeper ways with those who are different by virtue of their color, race, ethnic background, values and life experiences. White students who attend HBCUs have more frequent interactions with minorities and report more positive relationships with less fear, anxiety and reluctance. Having day-to-day group socialization toward a common goal of achieving an education provides a haven to improve race relations before entering the real world (Cartwright, 1996).

Further noted is that 56% of blacks who graduated from HBCUs go on to earn advanced degrees, including law, medicine and business. The retention rates for HBCU students attending graduate school are somewhat higher than those for TWI students. Black HBCU students are more likely than TWI students to obtain a Ph.D. and less likely to leave a program without obtaining a degree (Barton, 1999). The demographic characteristics of Graduate Record

Exam students who have attended HBCUs are not unusually disproportionate, while those who attended TWIs are disproportionately white, suggesting that each type of school better serves the ethnic group that it has traditionally served. The fact that the HBCU students are of lower socioeconomic status than the TWI students also suggests that the HBCUs provide an avenue for students with humble origins to pursue graduation. Consequently, they are more likely to be citizens who are actively engaged in the mainstream of America through community, church, government, civic, business and political affairs (Barton, 1999). In addition, black men and women along with Hispanic or Latino graduates of selective colleges (HBCUs) are more active than white graduates in entering into political, civic and community service work (Bowen, 1998). This benefits society overall as well as the emerging and new larger minority Hispanic-Latino middle classes.

Evidence Justifying the Continuance vs. Discontinuance of Jackson State University

The notion of "educational justification" of HBCUs, and Jackson State University in particular, involves identifying educational benefits these schools would offer that do not exist at TWIs. Therefore, the continuance or discontinuance of Jackson State University can be best addressed and answered by assessing the overall inferences from both the quantitative and the qualitative data obtained in this study.

Quantitatively speaking, Jackson State University has many issues of concern. The study initially sought to analyze JSU's institutional effectiveness in terms of key performance indicators: (a) mission assignments, (b) admission enrollment and headcounts, (c) graduation rates or degrees conferred, and (d) instructional programs. Afterwards, the study looked at the internal perceptions of employees of Jackson State University who went through the desegregation process to understand the impact of desegregation on the institution and explore if the input or evidence from this experience could justify the institution's continued existence.

The data in this study suggest that there continue to be strong arguments and empirical evidence for the continued existence of HBCUs and, certainly, Jackson State University. This institution, like other HBCUs, has continued to demonstrate that it is uniquely able to produce African-American leadership in various professions and fields. In non-traditional and underrepresented fields, JSU continues to produce a significant share of this nation's African-American graduates.

The data further indicate that although the numbers are not dominant, JSU, as compared to Mississippi's TWIs, is still able to prepare students successfully for graduate schools and professions. Jackson State University also provides a track record for producing African-Americans for leadership roles in their communities and for entrance into the local, state and national job markets. JSU is just as successful, and in many cases more successful, in preparing students for careers in engineering, science and business as Mississippi's TWIs. Not to be overlooked or understated is that the data also show JSU, like other HBCUs, has African-American students who are more likely to choose a major in academic science and business. White students who attend JSU, like those who attend other HBCUs, are more likely to choose a major in a para-profession versus a science. African-Americans who attend Mississippi's TWIs were less likely to choose natural, mathematical and biological sciences as majors and more likely to choose traditional majors in the fields of education and social work, etc. All of these findings are crucial because they explain the reality that JSU, as an HBCU, produces graduates in many underrepresented professions and fields. These findings are also consistent with both national and historical trends among students who attend HBCUs.

In summary, it is important to recognize that this study brought to light a larger picture of related issues and perspectives to the overall state of HBCU desegregation, race relations and society in America. These issues warrant further evaluation. Jackson State University appears to reflect its existence as a microcosm of a larger racially divided society. The development of black colleges and universities parallels the development of America's progressions and retrogressions from the stated ideals of achieving the American dream. There are those at Jackson State University who have fully embraced assimilation and are not impaired by a vision to make the institution less racially identifiable. Their optimism is seen in their desire to obtain resources to advance the institution, by any means necessary, into the same technological age enjoyed Mississippi's TWIs. The future of Jackson State University may very well embrace a multi-ethnic community that simply mirrors social behavior, attitudes and a student population reflective of the state and the union.

There is an element of Jackson State University that appears poised to validate and substantiate or justify its existence because it serves as the historical vanguard of African-American culture. This is a benefit that Mississippi's TWIs do not provide. No amount of money, policy changes and programs will deny the presence of African-Americans in Mississippi who desire to socialize and sustain their relationship with Jackson State University. On one hand, Jackson

State University may have to do very little because familiarity breeds contentment. Thus, African-American Mississippians see Jackson State University as their institution. They recognize that JSU may only continue to embrace cultural and racial diversity (the inclusion of more whites to the extent that whites feel more comfortable and secure on campus). For many at this institution, Jackson State University has to do only what it has done in the past. On the other hand, the threat of closure, merger and/or massive change poses a serious threat. Many of Jackson State University's employees and constituents are aware of HBCUs and their financial dilemmas. They are also keenly aware that powers beyond them must recognize and support their right to exist and offer a viable education to the citizens of Mississippi, regardless of color.

Equally relevant is the fact there exists a continual historical and present-day struggle over the existence of JSU. At the heart of the matter, not clearly seen in the quantitative data but reflected in the qualitative data, is the issue of what is important to each key player. For the Court and the legislature bodies, the issue is: Justify your existence as a single-race institution and enforce that institution's responsibility as it relates to the state's constitution. The issue for the Mississippi's Council on Higher Learning is: How do you keep control and power over the state's HBCUs, specifically JSU, in terms of allowing them to continue to exist and limit their efforts of self-determination? This challenge encompasses battles over control and restrictions that define missions, programs, accesses, budgets, constituents, institutional autonomy and governance, etc. For Jackson State University and other HBCUs, the issue is continued existence, funding, maintaining tradition, serving African-Americans and gaining respect equal to Mississippi's TWIs. For the constituents, they simply want a quality education at a quality price and support systems that an HBCU can provide to ensure their academic success and future professional opportunities.

This study further revealed that Jackson State University, like other HBCUs, is put on a short leash and told what to do, how to do it and, if you don't achieve the state-mandated standards, then the following will occur: (a) budget cuts, (b) restrictive funding, (c) dismantlement, (d) redefined missions, and (e) erosion of significant numbers of blacks and the emergence of more whites. In contrast, Mississippi's TWIs either have no leash or a much longer leash with unlimited flexibility involving academic freedom, governance and educational ventures. HBCUs, on the other hand, do not know academic freedom and governance in the true sense of the word. They also are not allowed to give any significant relevant input into the state's polices and discussions that determine their continued existence. If input is allowed, it seems less valued based on the interview data obtained.

Finally, despite the current predicament that Jackson State University and other HBCUs find themselves in, this study reflected that JSU has developed unique strengths and carried on an important mission. In providing services to students whose pre-college education was of poor quality, JSU and other HBCUs have developed special abilities to meet the needs of disadvantaged (primarily African-American) and non-traditional students (primarily white). They have also served, and continue to serve, as archives of African-American history, culture, values and contributions. They continue to serve, as they have done historically, as centers for the study of African-Americans and their urban, economic and social problems as well as achievements. HBCUs also offer something that TWIs don't. They serve as interpreters of African-American aspirations and experiences. The investigation and results of this study suggest there is a welcoming environment at JSU, like at many HBCUs where African-Americans can develop their skills and abilities. They can learn to better understand themselves and the society in which they live. Students, adults and non-traditional students can benefit in many additional ways from a predominantly black educational setting of their choice, namely: greater self-esteem; higher faculty expectations for their success; a greater number of positive black role models on campus; and a social climate receptive to race, color, gender and diverse economic backgrounds.

Recommendations for Further Research

In order for Jackson State University to clearly define a role for the twenty-first century and justify its continued existence based on educational effectiveness, the data obtained in this study suggest several key strategies. The following recommendations are presented for consideration by this institution and other HBCUs which desire a continued role in the twenty-first century.

1. Moderately diversify and actively increase the enrollment of non-African-American students while maintaining a significant percentage of African-American students.

2. Continue to serve as vanguards or archival institutions for African-American culture and history.

3. Restructure HBCU missions and educational programs to ensure their viability and educationally justifiable existence.

By using moderate diversification policies, public HBCUs could continue to play a significant role in educating African-Americans, satisfy the *Fordice* standard by discontinuing policies perpetuating racial identifiability and satisfy the integration philosophy underlying *Brown*. The benefits consequent to such a direction or action will be far-reaching.

Increasing the number of white students at public HBCUs will diminish criticism of these institutions because white students will also experience the benefits enjoyed by their black counterparts. The avenue is opened for white students (traditional and non-traditional) and especially white males, to develop stronger, positive self-concepts because they are forced to learn the value of earning the approval of others and co-participate in learning on a relatively level playing field, thus diminishing the need to have complete authority, power and control over the behavior, work ethic and socialization of non-whites. Increasing diversity at HBCUs via students, programs, activities, events, community partnerships and social programs may also increase interracial harmony between whites and blacks for a greater society.

By continuing the tradition of recording the historical contributions of African-Americans in the arts, humanities, education, law, medicine, sciences, community, civic and social affairs, etc., HBCUs can remain vanguards or archival institutions for African-American culture and history. Their continuing existence will ensure the authenticity of the "black experience" for present and future generations.

The third recommendation is offered based upon the findings in this study because it allows HBCUs to circumvent any unfavorable interpretations of *Fordice*. Public HBCUs exist because of prior *de jure* segregated systems enunciated in *Plessy* v. *Ferguson,* Due to *Plessy* v. *Ferguson's* separate but equal standard, most HBCUs are structured in a manner similar to Mississippi's in *Fordice,* For example, most public HBCUs are located in close proximity to and have duplicate, or dual, education programs similar to those offered by nearby, majority institutions. This, of course, has made it almost literally impossible for HBCUs to adhere to *Fordice's* "unnecessary duplication" standard and to establish that they do not have a dual, segregated system, because that is precisely why these HBCUs were originally founded.

There is, however, one way that states operating public HBCUs can elude *Fordice's* "unnecessary duplication" standard and that is by restructuring their university system so that public HBCUs do not have the same mission or educational programs as majority institutions located nearby. Of particular importance and inclusion should be a deliberate and direct effort by HBCUs to seriously focus on offering specific programs in underrepresented areas or fields for minorities. Such underrepresented areas or fields would include engineering, science, business, medicine, physics, chemistry and healthcare, etc. The end result could be an embracing of informational technology and an avenue for African-Americans to participate in the globalization of the economy, international affairs and domestic issues of paramount importance.

In conclusion, the continued existence of HBCUs does not constitute a threat to racial equality because these colleges and universities are open to members of all racial and ethnic groups. Just as other specialized institutions—such as religious colleges and women's colleges—HBCUs provide a choice for those seeking an educational environment consistent with their personal values and experiences. If these institutions are open to all applicants regardless of race, color, religion or ethnicity, etc., then they enhance equality and expand opportunities for blacks without restricting the options of others.

Finally, there must be more research done on HBCUs in the areas of governance, autonomy and policy issues that relate to an institution's role and responsibilities to continue to exist with some viable role and with some viable mission. Most importantly, a follow-up study should be done on JSU within 5 or 10 years relative to benchmarks and standards that explore Jackson State University's progress since the *Fordice* ruling.

Appendix

Interview Questions

1. How would you describe the impact of desegregation on Jackson State University in aterms of:

   a. admissions,

   b. student population,

   c. administrator/faculty composition,

   d. day to day social interactions between the races,

   e. finances,

   f. instructional programs, and

   g. support services.

2. What is your typical profile of a student attending JSU in terms of race, residence, degree aspiration and level of preparation for college?

3. Why do students choose JSU v. TWIS in Mississippi?

4. How do students at differ at JSU v. TWIS in Mississippi?

5. What is the dropout the rate of students in terms of race, background, classification, academic performance?

6. How does the retention rate at JSU compare with those students at TWIS in Mississippi?

7. What would you consider to be the strengths of JSU?

8. What does JSU offer that students cannot obtain or experience at TWIS?

9. What factors affect the dropout rate at JSU?

10. What is Jackson State University doing to address their problematic retention rate?

11. Has the university ever been penalized in terms of restrictions on state funding, negative accreditation report, etc."

12. What have been the funding differences between JSU and TWIS relative to faculty salaries, programs, facilities, financial aid, etc.?

13. What performance indicators or criteria are used by Jackson State University to measure or determine its own institutional effectiveness? The Mississippi Council on Higher Learning?

14. What do you feel is the public and private images of Jackson State University based on race in the state and specifically the immediate community?

15. How would you describe Jackson State University's relationship with the Council on Higher Learning and the State Legislature in general and over the years?

16. What were the findings of your recent SACS Accreditation Review?

17. How does the mission of JSU compare with those of the TWIS? How are you really different? Have there been any major or significant changes in your mission over the last two decades since the desegregation litigation begin?

18. If your students are not academically well-prepared when they enter JSU, then what measures are put into place to ensure student retention and student success?

19. How would you describe black-white relationships on campus and in the community between administrators, faculty, staff, students, and the general public?

20. What resources do you have that identify students at risk?

21. Is student retention a core issue at JSU? If so, in what context?

22. In what ways is JSU significant or vital to the state of Mississippi, and its immediate community?

23. What would you say is your greatest contributions in terms of quality and quantity at JSU?

24. What is JSU doing or has it done in terms of ensured racial diversity?

25. What is JSU doing or has it done in terms of acquiring quality faculty and faculty retention?

26. Since Jackson State University has been designated as the "Urban Institution" in Mississippi, do you feel it is serving its purpose adequately and effectively? If not, then why?

27. What obstacles, barriers and challenges have JSU had to overcome and/or may still be unresolved?

28. What do you feel is the future role of JSU?

29. What is JSU own internal perceptions about the desegregation experience? How do people really feel about the litigation?

30. What do people feel was the real injustice to JSU over the years?

31. What are the perceptions of the physical campus and facilities at JSU?

32. Would JSU have greater and higher degree completions and more quality learning if the institution was better funded with monies, programs, resources, support, services and facilities?

33. Why do a lot of students enter JSU but not graduate?

34. Why does JSU have a dismal graduate rate (19. 4 %) compared with its sister HBCU, Mississippi Valley State University (66.8 %?

35. How can JSU be the largest and most funded HBCU in Mississippi and have the lowest graduation rate?

36. Do you feel the Mission of JSU is clearly articulated and being achieved?

37. Is JSU penalized by the State for poor degree completion and graduation rates?

38. Who supports and does not support the President's vision, leadership and direction in which JSU is being led?

REFERENCES

Adams v. Richardson, 430 F. Supp. 118 (D.D. C. 1978).

Adarand v. Pena, 132 L. Ed. 2d 158 (1994).

Adarand Constructors, Inc. v. Mineta, 534 U.S. 103 (2001).

Alexander v. Holmes County Board of Education, 369 U.S. 19 (1969).

Allain v. Ayers, 674 F. Supp. 1523 N.D. Miss. (1987).

Allen, W. R. (1992). The color of success: African-American college student outcomes at predominantly white and historically black colleges and universities. *Harvard Educational Review, 62,* 26-44.

Allen, W. R. & N. Z. Haniff. (1991). Race, gender and academic performance in U.S. higher education. In W. R. Allen, E. G. Epps & N. Z. Haniff (Eds.), *College in black and white: African American students in predominantly white and historically black public universities* (pp. 95-110). Albany, NY: SUNY Press.

Altbach, J. (1991, September 27). Social support networks and undergraduate student academic success-related outcomes: A comparison of black and white students. *The Chronicle of Higher Education,* A46.

Anderson, J. D. (2001, July 14). Witness testimony excerpt—U.S. v. Fordice. *Ole Miss Gazette,* p. 23.

Anderson, J. D., (1999, Jan.-Feb.). Fordice: Perspectives on integration. *Academe, (1)3.*

Anderson, J. D., (1999). Colleges and universities, historically black, in the United States. *Encarta Africana.*

Anderson, J. D. (1988). *The education of blacks in the south, 1860-1935.* Chapel Hill, NC: The University of North Carolina Press.

Anderson, J. D. (1984). The schooling and achievement of black children: Before and after Brown v. Topeka, 1900-1980. In M. L. Maehr & D. Bartz (Eds.], *The effects of school desegregation on motivation and achievement* (pp. 103-121). Greenwich, CT: JAI Press.

Anonymous. (2003, April). Jackson State University: Education in the classroom and beyond. *Clarion Ledger.*

Astin, A. (1996). *Degree attainment rates at American colleges and universities: Effects of race, gender and institution type.* Los Angeles: Higher Education Research Institute.

Ayers v. Allain, 674 F. Supp. 1523, 1564 (N.D. Miss. 1987).

Barthelemy, S. J. (1984). The role of black colleges in nurturing leadership. In A. Garibaldi (Ed.) *Black colleges and universities: Challenges for the future* (pp. 14-25). New York: Praeger.

Barton, P. E. (1999). *Students at historically black colleges and universities: Their aspirations and accomplishments.* Princeton, NJ: Educational Testing Service.

Baxter, F. (1982, January). The institution of higher education: Defining the role of the traditional black college. *Journal of Law and Education, (11)1.*

Blumenstyk, G. (1991). Justice Department affirms federal backing for black colleges. *Chronicle of Higher Education, (28)8.*

Board of Education of Oklahoma v. Dowell, (1991). Bob Jones v. United States (1983).

Bochner, K. (1994). Qualitative methodology in social research. *Qualitative Sociology, (19)1,* 11-33.

Bond, H. (1934). *The education of the Negro in the American social order.* New York: Prentice Hall.

Bowen, W. G. & Bok, D. (1998). *The shape of the river: Long term consequences of considering race in college university admissions.* Princeton University Press.

Brotherton, P. (2001, June 7). Minority bachelor's degrees on the rise: Number of African-American bachelor's degree holders tops 100,000. *Black Issues in Higher Education.*

Brown v. Board of Education, Topeka, Kansas I, 347 U.S. 483 (1954). Brown v. Board of Education, Topeka, Kansas E, 349 U.S. 294 (1955).

Bullock, H. A. (1967). *A history of Negro education in the South from 1619 to the present.* Cambridge, MA: Harvard University Press.

Burgess, R. G. (Ed.). (1992). *Field research source book and field manual.* London: Allen and Unwin.

Bush Sr., G. W. (1991). *White house initiatives on black colleges and universities.* Washington, D.C.

Butler, G. L. (1994). Legal and policy issues in higher education. *Journal of Negro Education, (63)3.*

Cage, M. C. (1990). Sharp tensions accompany new role for historically black Bowie State University. *Chronicle of Higher Education, (38)4.*

Carter, D. & Wilson, R. (1995, March). Thirteenth annual status report on minorities in higher education. *American Council on Education.*

Cartwright, J. (1996). Race relations on campus. *Chronicle of Higher Education, (37)4* Carvenale, R. (1999). History of desegregation education. *Academe, (70)24.* The Civil Rights Act, 42 Y,S,C, 2000 to 2000d-4a. (1964).

Cohen, J. & Rendall, S. (1994). Limbaugh: A colored man who has a problem with color? *Fairness and Accuracy in Reporting.* Available online at: http://www.fair.org/articles/limbaugh-color.html.

Coleman, C. (1990). History of desegregation education. *Academe, (70)24.*

Constantine, Hill M. (1994). The added value of historically black colleges. *Academe, (80)3.*

Cooper v. Aaron, 358 U.S. 1 (1958).

Davis, R. B. (1996). Blacks and higher education. *Harvard Educational Review, 53,* 34-78.

Davis, R. B. (1991). *Social support networks and educational outcomes at historically black colleges.* Albany: SUNY Press.

DeLoughry, T. J. (1991). Washington update: President lashes out at critics of his policies on education. *Chronicle of Higher Education, (38)4.*

Draden, J. T. & Hargett, S. (1981). Historically black colleges and the dilemma of desegregation. *Integrated Education, 19,* 3-6.

Evans, A. L., Evans, V., Jackson, A.M., (2002). Historically black colleges and universities (HBCUs), *Education, (123)1.*

Fletcher, M. A. (2001, April 24). Miss, desegregation suit settled for $500 million: Mississippi settlement ends lengthy battle. *Washington Post.*

Franklin, D. (1990, Summer). Predicting black achievement among white culture in higher education. *Journal of Negro Education,* 319-325.

Garibaldi, A. M. (1991). The role of historically black colleges in facilitating resilience among African American students. *Education and Urban Society, (24)*1.

Garibaldi, A. M. (1984). Black colleges: An overview. In A. Garibaldi (Ed.), *Black colleges and universities for the future,* (pp. 3-9). New York: Praeger.

Gentemann, B. (1989, Jan.-Feb.). Methods and modes of institutional assessment. *Community College Journal of Research and Practice, (20)*1, 75-85.

Goes v. Board of Education of Knoxville, Tennessee, 373 U.S. 683 (1963).

Gray, W. (2000). Contributions of the black college. *Chronicle of Higher Education, (42)*5.

Green v. New Kent County School Board, 391 U.S. 430 (1968).

Griffin v. Prince Edward Co. Board of Education VA, (1964).

Grutter v. Bollinger, 288F.3rd 732 (6th Circuit, 2002).

Guernsey, L. (1996). Federal court orders Mississippi's historically black colleges to raise their admissions standards. *Chronicle of Higher Education, (42)*29.

Gurin, P. & Katz, D. (1966). *Motivation and aspiration in the Negro college.* Ann Arbor, MI: Survey Research Center.

Hawkins, D. (1995). AAUP report finds HBCU role essential to higher education. *Black Issues in Higher Education, (11)*24.

HCC. (2001). *Holmes Community College: 1999-2001 fact book.* Mississippi. Author. Available online at: http://www.holmescc.edu/IE/factbook/mississipidata.htm.

Healy, P. (1996). Courts hear arguments in Miss, desegregation case. *Chronicle of Higher Education, (11)*43.

Healy, P. (1966, April 26). Myriad of problems for black colleges. *Chronicle of Higher Education,* A31-A36.

Hebel, S. (2001). A new push to integrate public black colleges. *Chronicle of Higher Education, (47)24.*

Henderson, K. (2003). Statistical facts and black achievement. *Academe,* (32)84.

Historically black colleges and universities and higher education desegregation. (1991, March). U.S. Department of Education Office for Civil Rights. Washington, D.C. 2002-1100.

Historically black colleges and universities: A future in the balance. (1995, Jan.-Feb.). *Academe, (81)*1,49-58.

Hoffman, C. M., Synder, T. D., & Sonneberg, B. (1992). *Historically black colleges and universities, 1976-1990,* Washington, D.C: National Center for Education Statistics.

Hoffman, C.M., et. al. (1995). Shifting gears: College enrollment and desegregation. *Change, (25)*1.

Hopwood v. Texas, 861 F. Supp. 51 (1996).

Houton, T. (1996). Institutional effectiveness and benchmarks. *Qualitative Research, (1)3.*

Hughes, C E. (1992). A case for the formation of strategically focused consortia among HBCUs. *Journal of Negro Education, (61)4.*

Institution of Higher Learning Information Management System State of Mississippi 1995-2002: Headcounts, admissions, academic programs, degree completions, race, gender and residence.

Jaschik, S. (1999). High court takes up desegregation case. *Chronicle of Higher Education, (97)25.*

Jaschik, S. (1995). Excerpts from judge's decision in Mississippi desegregation case. *Chronicle of Higher Education, (41)4%.*

Jaschik, S. (1995). Excerpts from judge's ruling on desegregating Alabama colleges. *Chronicle of Higher Education, (41)4%.*

Jaschik, S. (1995). Justice Thomas stresses the role of predominantly black colleges. *Chronicle of Higher Education, (41)4\.*

Jaschik, S. (1994). Victory for black colleges. *Chronicle of Higher Education,* (40)21.

Jaschik, S. & Meyer, J. (1992). Public black colleges face new pressures. *Chronicle of Higher Education, (38)45.*

Jaschik, S. (1991). Legal and philosophical position of public black colleges at a watershed as high court takes up desegregation case. *Chronicle of Higher Education, (41)\.*

Jaschik, S. (1991). Justices appear split as high court hears desegregation cases: Future of black colleges at stake in appeal on Mississippi's policy. *Chronicle of Higher Education, (41)*1.

Jones, H. & Richards-Smith, H. (1987). Historically black colleges and universities: A force in developmental education part II. *Research in Developmental Education,* Appalachian State University, *(4)5.*

Keys v. School District I, 413 U.S. 189 (1973).

Knopp, L. (1995). *Women in higher education today: A mid-1990's profile.* American Council on Education Research Brief.

Lee v. Macon County Board of Education, 267 F. Supp. 458 (M.D. Ala. 1967). Lemelle, C. (2002, July 2). *Interview on HBCUs with A. L. Evans.* Houston, Texas.

Lemelle, T. J. (2002, Fall). Historically black colleges and universities yesterday, today and tomorrow. *Education, (123)1,* 70-190.

LaRouche, J. (1976, December). Institutional effectiveness in higher education. *American Journal of Community Colleges, 21,* 34-38.

Maxwell, J. (1996). *Qualitative themes in research.* Chicago: University of Chicago Press.

Medley, D. K. (1994). Black access to education and college achievement. *Negro Educational Review, 49,* 9-22.

Mercer, J. (1994). A crusader for the survival of historically black colleges. *Chronicle of Higher Education, (41)4.*

Mercer, J. (1994). Kentucky law requires progress on desegregation. *Chronicle of Higher Education, (41)2.*

Mercer, J. (1994). Southern states consider freezing programs until cases are decided. *Chronicle of Higher Education, (41)2.*

McLaurin v. Regents of Oklahoma, 339 U.S. 637 (1950).

Merriam, S. B. (1988). *Case study research in education. A qualitative approach.* San Francisco: Jossey-Bass Publishers.

Miliken v. Bradley I, (1974).

Miliken v. Bradley II, 433 U.S. 267 (1977).

Mishler, J. (1991). *Themes and theories in qualitative research.* Chicago: The University of Chicago Press.

Missouri ex rel. Gaines v. Canada, 305 U.S. 337 (1938).

Monroe v. Board of Commissioners of the City of Jackson, 395 U.S. 225 (1968).

Morgan v. Kerrigan, 401 F. Supp 215 (D. Mass. 1975).

Morris, V. (1981). A history of black college education. *Journal of Higher Education, 68,* 544-549.

Mydrall, P. (1944). *The American dilemma.* New York: Crown.

Myers, J. (1989, October). Desegregation and black colleges. *Chronicle of Higher Education, 45,* A-34-36.

NACME. (2002). *Higher education.* Author. Available online at: http://www.nacme.org/rsch/data/highered.html

National Collegiate Athletic Association. (2002). *National collegiate athletic association: 2001 graduation rates report.* Author.

Norris v. State Council on Higher Education, 327 F. Supp. 1368 (E.D. Va. 1971). O'Brien, H. (1999). The evolution of black colleges. *Journal of Higher Education, (54)65.*

Office for Civil Rights. (1991). *Report on postsecondary education in America.* Washington, D.C.

Offices of Finance and Administration. *Institution of Higher Learning Annual Report 1991-2001.*

Office of Research and Planning. *Institution of Higher Learning State of Mississippi Publication 1995-2002.*

Okoye, R. (2003, May 20). *Personal interview.* Jackson State University, Jackson, Mississippi.

PBS. (1997). Opening doors, opening minds. *Online News Hour.* Available online at: http://www.pbs.org/newshour/forum/october97/rock5.html.

Phillip, M. (1992). *Desegregation cases black and white. In pursuit of equality in higher education* (pp. 105-110). Dix Hills, NY: General Hall Inc.

Plessy v. Ferguson, 163 U.S. 537 (1896).

Raney v. Board of Education of the Gould School District, 391 U.S. 433 (1968).

Regents of University of California, vs. Bakke, 438 U.S. 265 at 317 (1978).

Renner, K. E. (1998, March-April). Redefining the issue of racial preference: Minority access to higher education. *Change.*

Rhodes, P. J. (1992). Black colleges and universities. *Negro Educational Review, 48,* 18-22.

Richards-Smith, J. V., (1987). *Public and private black colleges.* Boston: Allyn and Bacon. Riddick v. School Board of the City of Norfolk, Virginia, (1986).

Roebuck, J. B. & Murty, K. S. (1993). *Historically black colleges and universities: Their place in American higher education,* Westport, CT: Prager.

Ryan, C. (1999). *Qualitative research for education. An introduction to theory and methods.* Boston: Allyn and Bacon.

Sanders v. Ellington, 288 R Supp. 937 (M.D. Tenn 1968).

Sawyer, P. (2003, April 2). Musgrove shoots down budget bill. *Clarion Ledger.*

Sipuel v. Board of Regents Univ. of Oklahoma, 332 U.S. 631 (1948).

Smith, W. G. (1994). Diversity works: The emerging picture of how students benefit. *National Journal of Sociology, 2,* 3-33.

Smith, A. W. (1991). Personal traits, institutional prestige, racial attitudes and African-American student academic performance in college. In W. R. Allen, E. G. Epps & N. Z. Haniff (Eds.). *College in black and white: African-American students in predominantly white and historically black public universities,* (pp. 111-126). Albany, SUNY Press.

Solutions Advancing People, Inc. (2003). Jackson State University. Available online at: http://www.universities.com/Schools/J/Jackson_State_University.asp.

Sowell, T. (1989). *Choosing a college: A guide for parents and students.* Harper & Row Publishers.

Spence, M. M. (1993). Affirmative action at mid life: A proponent's agenda for the 90's. *Change, (25)*1.

State of Florida ex rel. v. Board of Control, 350 U.S. 413 (1956).

Stefokovich, J. A & Leas, T. (1994). A legal history of desegregation in higher education. *Journal of Negro Education, (63)3.*

Swann v. Charlotte-Mecklenburg Board of Education, supra 402 U.S. 1 (1971). Sweatt v. Painer, 339 U.S. 629 (1950).

Tate, D. (1999, June 14). Diversity and destruction in higher education. *Black College Monthly.*

Thomas, G. & Hill, S. (1987). Black institutions in U.S. higher education: Present roles, contributions, future projections. *Journal of College-Student Personnel. (28)6.*

Tinto, V. (1990). *Leaving college: Rethinking the causes and cures of student attrition. (2^n ed.).* Chicago, IL: The University of Chicago Press.

Todd, T. (1998). Institutional effectiveness at two-year colleges: The southern region of the United States. *Community College Review, (26)3,* 57-56.

Tollett, K. (1994). The fate of minority based institutions after Fordice: An essay. *Review of Litigation, 13,* 447.

Trent, W. T., (1991). Focus on equity: Race and gender differences in degree attainment, 1975-76; 1980-81. In W. R. Allen, E. G. Epps & N. Z. Haniff (Eds.), *College in black and white: African-American student in predominantly white and historically black public universities* (pp. 41-59). Albany: SUNY Press.

United States v. Alabama, 628 F. Supp. 1137 (N.D. Ala., 1983). United States v. Fordice, et. al, 50 U.S. 120 L Ed. 2d 575 (2002). United States v. Louisiana, 692 F. Supp. 642 (E.D. La., 1993). United States v. Montgomery County Board, 395 U.S. 225 (1969).

Wagener, U. & Smith, E. E. (1993). Maintaining a competitive edge: Strategically planning for historically black institutions. *Change, (25)*1.

Walden, J. C. (1988). Desegregation of higher education in Alabama unresolved. *Education Law Report,* 505.

Waltman, J. (1994). Assuring the future of black colleges. *Chronicle of Higher Education, (40)44.*

Ware, L. (1994). Will there be a different world after Fordice? *Academe, (80)3.*

Wayne State University. (2001, September). *Affirmative action status report: 2000-2001.* Wayne State University Board of Governors.

Weaver, F. (1992). Black public colleges and universities: A review of institutional option. *Journal of Black Studies, (22)4.*

Weinberg, M. (1977). *Minority students: A research appraisal.* Washington, D.C.: National Institute of Education.

Wenglinksky, H. H. (1997). Educational justification of historically black colleges and universities: A policy response to the U.S. Supreme Court. *Educational Evaluation and Policy Analysis, (18)1,* 91-103.

Wilson, R. (1990). Can black colleges solve the problem of access for black students? *American Journal of Education, (98)4.*

Woodson, C. (1919). *The education of the Negro prior to 1861.* Washington, D.C.: Associated Publishers.

Wyatt, J. C. (1997). Mississippi higher education issues. *Mississippi Journal of Law, (34)18,73-89.*

Yates, W. T. (1993). Equity management: Affirmative action for the 21st century. *Change, (28)1.*

Yin, R. (1994.) *Case study research, design and methods (2nd Ed.).* Newbury Park: Sage Publications.

ABOUT THE AUTHOR

Dr. Eric O. Rogers Author,
Educator, Psychologist, Pastor, Social Critic

Eric 0. Rogers, Ph.D., is a native of Earlington, Kentucky and calls Nashville, Tennessee his adopted home. The fourth born of five children and the youngest son of the late Dallas Minor Rogers, Sr., and the late Bernice King Rogers (of Earlington, Kentucky), he makes his current home in St. Louis, Mo.

He holds a **Bachelor of Science Degree** in Psychology (Tennessee State University, Nashville, Tennessee) and received a **Master's Degree** in Psychology (Harvard University, Cambridge, Mass.) Furthermore, he earned a **Ph.D.** from the University of Kentucky. He is currently involved in Postdoctoral Study at Harvard University and theological study at Dallas Theological Seminary, Dallas, Texas.

Furthermore, Dr. Rogers began his professional career as a Marketing Consultant for the Transmerica Corporation in our nation's capital, Washington, D.C. In addition, he has lived and worked in Boston, Massachusetts, New York, New York, Nashville, Tennessee and Louisville, Kentucky and has held numerous professional positions inclusive of the following: **Research Assistant, a Private School Teacher** and as a **Psychologist** in clinical practice (Nashville, Tennessee). Dr. Rogers has also served as an **Educational and Testing Consultant** for ACT(The American College Testing Service (Iowa City, Iowa) and the Educational Testing Service (Princeton, New Jersey) in which he administered standardized testing (SAT,GRE,LSAT,MCAT,DAT, NTE,etc.) He is also a former **Chief G.E.D. Administrator.**

Academically, he has served as a higher education administrator as **Director of Testing/Assessment** at Kentucky State University. Equally important, he is a former **Federal Officer** with the U.S. Department of Justice (EEOC-Equal Employment Opportunity Commission) in St. Louis, Missouri were he has investigated over 5,000 cases involving sex, sexual harassment, race, age and disability discrimination in the workplace (Missouri, Illinois, Iowa and Kansas). Furthermore, Dr. Rogers is a former "**Teacher of the Year**" recipient and has taught at various universities and colleges (University of Kentucky; Missouri Baptist University; Maryville University and St. Charles Community College).

In addition, Dr. Rogers is an **ordained Baptist minister** with the Southern Baptist Convention (Atlanta, Georgia) and the National Baptist Convention, USA (Nashville, Tennessee). He has served as Pastor of four churches spanning a 16-year ministry career. He currently pastors the St. Stephen Baptist Church, a multi-cultural and urban based metroplitan church located in St. Louis, Missouri.

A 20 year veteran in higher education and published author, **Dr. Rogers is a 2003 recipient in Who's Who Among America's Teachers.** Further, Dr. Rogers lectures nationwide on Multicultural Education, Race, Religion and African-American History and Culture. He serves on numerous professional boards and community organizations.

0-595-33274-9

www.ingramcontent.com/pod-product-compliance
Lightning Source LLC
Chambersburg PA
CBHW061311280526
45784CB00002B/956